Jamigrant: The Story of A Jamaican Immigrant

Jamigrant: The Story of A Jamaican Immigrant

Experiences through Immigration, the Justice System, and Teaching

MARIE BELL-MACK

For written correspondence, contact the Author at the following address:
PO Box 8109,
Pelham, N.Y. 10803
Copies are available on Amazon.com, Amazon European websites,
CreateSpace e-store, and bookstores.
Publication available in hardcopy and Kindle e-book. Title is available for
Standard and Expanded distribution.

Printed in paperback. First edition published 2016

ISBN-13: 9781535420990
ISBN-10: 1535420995
Library of Congress Control Number: 2016913676
CreateSpace Independent Publishing Platform
North Charleston, South Carolina

Acknowledgments

To my father, Eric, who still sees me as Daddy's little girl.
My stepmom, Evelyn, who reared me with
unconditional love.
In honor of my mother, Hyacinth, whose presence I
feel.
My siblings, who are all different and yet the same in
love to me.
And…
To my darling husband, Dewitt. Really, how much stronger can our love be?

Then:

To my gardener, Julio, an immigrant like myself. He
came here on November 22, 1969. He speaks Italian
in English, and I speak English and patois in Italian.
Together we communicate with nature and pride. My
beautiful gardens give me the inspiration to write.

Contents

Author's Note

*Your talent is God's gift to you. What you
do with it is your gift back to God.*
—LEONARDO BUSCAGLIA

Many times we read a quote, a poem, or a book, and
it resonates with us. It grabs us, and with a stick of
urgency, it wakes us and then beats us into a pulp of submission. That is the moment when we pause and think of
why the person who wrote such a message was sent into
our lives. And so I did, when one night I read the above
quote of Mr. Buscaglia. I wanted to know more about this
man and why God had sent him to deliver a message to
me. He haunted me even when I tried to sleep. He would
say, "Wake up; go write. Perfect your gift and give it back
to God."

When I checked on who the messenger was, I realized
it was no coincidence that he was chosen to bring the
message; we had a lot in common. Leo was born into a

family of immigrants, and he later became a teacher and, among other things, a writer.

And so, Leo, sitting in the clouds, from one immigrant to another, I thank you for annoying me in my sleep. You were only following God's direction. I'll perfect His gift and give it back to Him myself.

I woke up and wrote *Jamigrant* out of deep respect for Leo and my unwavering gratitude to God.

Prologue

This is an immigrant's story.

It can only be told as seen through the lens of a Jamigrant, powerful enough to magnify the experiences of all others who came to "the land of the free and the home of the brave" with similar intentions. There is no particular sequence to the events or order to the experiences shared. It is certain that we all have experienced or will experience some part of this story. You can say with derision, "Oh no, not me," or you can be honest, kick back, grasp the lessons inherent in all these common experiences, sigh or laugh, and simply go on, embracing the realization that there is no time to do over.

Let's face it: the decision to immigrate is one that is based partly on observing and imitating those who have gone before us. And although the decision is a challenging and sometimes confounding one, it is by far the easiest of any we will encounter.

That is, if we believe in the philosophical extracts of Confucius. Somewhere embedded in his many analects and quotes, he wrote that, "By three methods we may learn wisdom: First, by reflection, which is noblest; second, by imitation, which is easiest; and third, by experience, which is the bitterest." Using his teachings as a guide and then through *Jamigrant*, which is the story of myself as a Jamaican immigrant, I will have done the first: a true reflection of my journey thus far. The second was by far the easiest, thanks to those who came before me. The third, sharing my experiences that transformed me and enabled me to acquire wisdom and success, was by far the bitterest.

Personal life lessons were of the fall-brush-yourself-off-and-get-up type. I had seen much worse situations every time I met a challenge, so prayers, faith, endurance, and perseverance always helped me through. I had seen people in general, not just aliens, encounter difficulties, which made me reflect upon Bradford's wisdom: "There but for the grace of God go I."

Make no mistake: there were times when I told God, through ignorance and desperation, that if only He would help me just this one last time through a difficulty at hand or to regain my balance after I had slipped, I would never, ever bother Him again. Then suddenly, as I emerged out of the valley and, through ingratitude and forgetfulness, allowed my hand to slip out of His grasp, I suddenly realized once again that I can do nothing without Him holding my hand.

Also there were those days when, after breaking my promise to serve Him and sin no more, I questioned whether a moment of darkness was His punishment toward me for such a promise not kept. But once that darkness was erased by light and hope, I learned once more that His grace is genuine, and life's difficulties are not punishments devised by the most gracious God.

And yet, "Most days I pray, but some days I curse; some days I even put myself first. But it's not what I do, the cross made that clear." One thing of which I am certain is that "one day Jesus will call my name," regardless of the land in which I choose to settle.

The experiences I write of were ones gathered along my career path while working in the justice system and also while teaching as an adjunct professor of criminal justice. There were other jobs along the way that welcomed me as an immigrant in the true spirit of New York, where we first accept the job and then we are told what it is.

And so, for those who ponder the idea of immigrating, I owe the telling of this story to you. It is a tremendous gamble that we take in giving up the familiar for the unknown, trading the many things that are truly free for those we believe will sustain us. And as we enter each phase of life, we see that the things we traded are the only sustenance we truly needed. It's like a plant: once we uproot it and transfer it to new soil, we hope as gardeners that it will flourish and not wither away. As humans, age is a determinant in most things that we desire to do over. Test runs are luxuries of life that we must do early, quickly, and infrequently, by putting our roots down and trying hard to nourish and sustain them in soil that is carefully selected early in life.

The only time we become totally disappointed about life and living, wherever we may be, is when there is confusion and misinterpretation of what happiness and success really mean. We only truly succeed when, through sharing with others, we help them to avoid a mistake we have made or achieve an accomplishment we have experienced. And that we can do anywhere.

Happiness is seeing how much we have helped. The beauty of nature and its birds are free. If you have these things in abundance, cherish and enjoy them. Let every day count. You will spend some time, though not too much time, being "young and restless," and you can always remain "bold and beautiful," but "as the world turns," you must remember that there are tasks to be accomplished before you get some relaxation in a "little house on the prairie," someplace where you'll continue your "one life to live." Your shared experiences will help someone...if only to laugh.

Remember, we can never seek to reconstruct a person's life story. We can simply appreciate the teller's generosity of loaning it to us, to be used as a guide. Everyone has a unique story to tell. Be generous and brave; share yours.

Here is mine.

One

THE MONOCLED PROFESSION

In the summer of 1981, I began to realize and appreciate the true beauty of paradise and how much of it was free. The awe of the place was always there, but the nuances of high school life had deprived me of the maturity of inhaling the spectacular creation of the landscape: the blue hills standing protective guard like soldiers over the gentle streams and calm meandering rivers; the turquoise ocean, with its white sandy beaches dotted with seashells and with corals and treasures submerged in its bosom; the palatable culinary delights like escovitched fish and so on; the obedient animals; and a people with a language, culture, and music of our own.

To this day, I search in wonderment to decipher how some of the native vocabulary was derived from the English language. The words were so carefully crafted that they bear several meanings depending on the mere intonation used. Some words are clearly distortions of English words, while others are genius creations with meanings so peculiar and germane to the culture. "Bombo," for example, can be interpreted as an exclamation of shock, surprise, or awe when said in a loud manner. When said softly, with a drag on the last "O," it means, "I just can't believe this; it is too good or funny to be true." When used as a noun, it means any private part of the human anatomy in a derogatory manner. The dictionary of complete words is not the only unique component of patois. The pronunciation of certain letters is substituted for others as well. Notable among such substitutions is the letter "H," which periodically takes the place of "W" in many words. The word "wool," which is a type of material derived from sheep and not necessarily found in paradise, is pronounced as "hool," and "wood" is pronounced as "hood." The latter can be interpreted as vulgar and obscene when used in a certain context. A delicious staple such as Whole Wheat Bread, when pronounced in the dialect, would imply that the bread was in a serious state of decay, not worthy of consumption.

Suffice it to say, the creation of patois was so remarkable, intriguing, and funny that a good theatrical production, preceded by a well-penned literary piece, should be composed in its honor and recognition. Someone needs to compose a long play and a book detailing its creation.

That summer, I remember, was my first out of high school, in preparation for a journey along the path of tertiary advancement. There was no choice of which institution to attend or what profession I would undertake, as the culture, at least during that time, weighed heavily on the decision of the father. He chose teaching for me, and so it was. Lest anyone should harbor any pity that such a life choice having been made by the father for a child equates to psychological abuse, let me spend a few seconds to dissuade your fears. Dr. Philgood is certainly not needed. I am fine—no childhood trauma or anything.

Jamaican society at the time was deeply entrenched in patriarchy. It was a social system in which men held primary power. A residue of this may still linger there, but it is not widespread and is quarantined in a very remote area of the island. We have come a long way, well-traveled and liberated.

Under this old system of patriarchal rule, the father made decisions when such decisions related to social privileges; anything to do with politics and what political party or principles to support; when and from what family lines boyfriends could be courted—and he had moral authority even in cases where he himself transgressed; and so on and so forth. That was all we were accustomed to; that was all we knew.

What was strange, though, was that in the absence of the father, the grandmother possessed full authority and jurisdiction over everything, even the God that you served. And stranger yet was the fact that there were situations in which the father had two households, one with a wife and one with a sweetheart, and both sets of children played together harmoniously at school and took care of one another. It was not uncommon to see both women exchanging pleasantries in the street on their way to the marketplace.

I share no responsibility in the creation of this system; I'm only reporting that it was in existence before gradually being phased out. I am also happy to report that most of the children who were exposed to this system have turned out extraordinarily well.

Despite this system being frowned upon or misunderstood in other societies, it certainly had its advantages. Due to its existence, there was no bullying tolerated at school. Cyber bullying was non-existent as there was no cyber space. We enjoyed physical space with face to face interactions. But this unique system of familial ties, ensured that in the event anyone was being picked on, the other twelve children who were half siblings to the one being jeered, would bring an abrupt end to such a situation. The prospective bully would be told by the flock that "we have the same puppa, aho!" This statement helps to emphasize the depth, acceptance, and strength of the patriarchal culture at the time.

"Aho," translated, means "let me enlighten you, in case you were unaware." Notice its position at the end of the statement. "Aho" is never placed anywhere other than at the end of a sentence. Its strategic location solidifies the speaker's point and demonstrates passion and finality. The person being spoken to is forewarned by hearing "aho," and it becomes immediately understood that such a person is on the losing end of whatever stick is under question. It's like saying "period" at the end of a sentence, but ten times more passionately and on the brink of combat.

So now it's understood why, on a September morning in 1981 in the year of our Lord, in full compliance with my father's instruction, aho (or else), I was enrolled in the nearest teachers' college to home. The quarter mile proximity of the campus to the house spoke to his over-protective nature as a father and his inability to see me as anything other than Daddy's little girl. The veranda of the house, wrapped around its structure, inciden-tally provided access to a panoramic view of the college grounds.

The institution had a rule engraved in stone that teacher-students would reside on campus on lockdown. I am almost sure, though it's still hard to prove, that he must have tried to pull every string possible to override this stipulation and have me return home every night. For he knew many people and was socially well-connected within the community and beyond.

Campus life was blanketed with intense oversight, and strict adherence to both intellectual discipline and moral uprightness was vigorously enforced. Academic and social survival on the compound was grueling, but the advancement of time, sound academic standing, and ultimate transformation into virtuosity made me an acceptable candidate for continued study and inclusion within the program.

I met, mingled, and studied with students from all walks of life and from all fourteen parishes in paradise. To this day, numerous bonds have survived from those years, and there are few that the passing of time or the distance of continents have been successful in dissolving. So much emphasis was placed on discipline that it was impossible to separate the core curriculum from how we comported ourselves, even in the dining room on weekdays or the concert hall on weekends.

Modesty in attire was marked by conservative frocks for the ladies and slacks with well-pressed shirts for the men, who were few in enrollment, both specifically on campus and throughout the entire profession as well. Any sign of formfitting clothes, transparency in the material, slits or possible wardrobe malfunction in attire, was a sure indication that one had broken away from a decent upbringing, and was considered to be indicative of a lifestyle that was loose. Hence, for classes we wore uniforms to ensure a professional atmosphere in the classroom.

Complete abstinence from any form of sexual proclivity was hidden somewhere among the unwritten rules. Respect and conformity started each day, as teacher-students stood when the professors entered the room. No one in their right frame of mind would dare to sit before being instructed to do so by the entering lecturer. Any object regardless of its size that dared to roll off the desk onto the floor would remain there until the conclusion of the delivery of the lecture. It was understood that the object had already created enough distraction by the noise it made upon contact with the ceramic tiled floor, and therefore, the clumsy owner of said object would not create any further diversion.

The teaching profession had been well-known for its population of predominantly dedicated, middle-aged women, whose trademark was the monocle that rested on their noses and their impeccable command of the English language. Their maturity and expertise were guaranteed by the fact that they entered the classrooms, first as untrained teachers, earned many years of experience, and then years later, through some vetting process still unclear to me, would formalize their position by attending teachers' college.

Not that they needed the formal training at this point, as they were true accomplished professionals in their own right. They were born to teach. It was in their blood, and they owned it. If these teachers taught you something and you failed to learn, it was due either to a lack of attention or you were in fact a dunce. They taught principles instead of mere lessons, so in actuality the fortunate population of students who were taught by them, could apply their knowledge to any given situation in academia and in life, for that matter. Communities relied on them for the shaping of their children, and parents would meet with them to discuss any matter whatsoever, which was affecting their children. These matters would range from serious health issues such as sleep apnea to inattentiveness and fidgeting. But regardless of the condition, parents relied on these veteran-teachers for a solution.

Students for example who showed signs of excessive day-time sleepiness, would be placed up-front and under the noses of these very observant teachers. In a short period of time with absolutely no intervention from a doctor or therapist, these affected children would be rid of their sleeping disorders. It wouldn't take long before a happy mother would be thanking the teacher that, "him doin' much betta." Soon there would be other parents being referred for treatment of their children with similar conditions. But the convenience we enjoyed of having a doctor, teacher and social worker all rolled-up into one, had slowly began to subside.

The early eighties marked one of the first batches of prospective teachers who, like me, commenced training immediately upon completing high school. This break in tradition, perhaps due to the perception, real or imagined, of immaturity and unearned status of us not getting our feet wet in the classroom setting, created a silent rift between the newcomers and the pacesetters. We were criticized for our lack of matrimonial or maternal commitments, because the idea of being a teacher had to be first tested with having the responsibility of managing your own household.

We had neither husbands nor children and, therefore, were just too new to teach anything we hadn't even begun to learn or experience ourselves. Our lack of financial acumen was another obstacle in our way, since our education was being funded by someone other than ourselves. We were deemed too privileged and *stush*, or show-off, to know what it meant to be humble, tempted, and tried.

Semester after semester for three arduous years, and one of internship inside a classroom, hard work under intense scrutiny paid off, and induction into the profession became a monumental achievement for me.

All the dreams regarding selective economic postulations were short-lived as a jolt of realization revealed how limited paradise was in terms of positions in the job market. Its majestic beauty stood in far contrast to its lack of economic resources.

Perseverance and a firmness of purpose made me accept my first teaching position in a tiny elementary school, located where no buses or taxis had gone before. The hills surrounding the school were the only sensuous representation of the heights I had attained. The valley in which the school was carefully nestled was a representation of the things that would later make me stronger in life. Valleys are important. They provide a spectacular juxtaposition to the mountains. We can't have one without the other. So had I known these words then, I would certainly have been humming, "Today I face a mountain that I have no *strength* to climb. Where I stand to the peak is a distance on my own I *cannot* reach…but this journey of a thousand miles begins right here on my *knees*."

My colleagues and I, having no other methods of transportation (barring a donkey or a horse), with which to get to this tiny elementary school to teach, hired a 1964 Ford Falcon station wagon, lime-green, with the rear end touching the road surface as it negotiated the curbs and hills morning after morning. She maneuvered the unpaved limestone roads, caressing the winding curves with her soft bald tires, entertaining her passengers with clunks and jolts at every turn. She gave no warning of an impending empty tank, as the needle inside the round glass gauge was no longer attached. A gradual crawl with a choking sound, followed by an abrupt halt, would be a sure sign that she had been deprived of petroleum and was thus too dehydrated to go on.

There were no gas stations around, so a bottle of gas with a piece of hose in it would be retrieved from the trunk to replenish her fluid line. Her musical phenomenon designed to warn of an impending collision was no longer operable. After all, that was a feature affixed to the center of her steering wheel where she was born. Such a device was not necessary in paradise, as the natives cherished the luxury to move at a relaxed pace. We wanted no blowing of anything to tell us how fast to move. To make haste in paradise was a sign that something was amiss with the person performing such an act. Later I learned that lack of haste, rush, and hurry in her birthplace was a sign of emotional instability and laziness. Smoke emanated with great flatulence from her muffler, which was tied to her undercarriage by a rope.

As the new passenger who needed so much to get to the children who relied on us day after day, I secured my place—the only place that was left for a passenger—between the two front seats located on top of the emergency brake lever, which was no longer covered by a padding of rubber. The absence of the rubber padding on the lever over which I had to sit can best be understood by anyone who dares to imagine the urgency it created in me wanting to get up. It was there that I sat each morning, enjoying the aroma from the kitchens of the folks who brewed chocolate and coffee and cooked fried dumplings and salt fish, sending the aroma whipping through the car windows as we drove to teach our classes.

I know I prayed daily for the weather to be in our favor, as the slightest arrival of rain would have created the need for us to wedge cardboard pieces between the windows and the doors to ward off any type of flooding, which our jalopy would find impossible to withstand. The handles that wound the windows up and down were represented by protruding rusty screws, and so the glass sat and rattled angrily in the frame of the door, serving no definitive purpose other than to annoy. She didn't care much about the soaking of the upholstery, as there was none left covering the yellowish-brown sponge, from the many years she had worked as the village hearse, and in between as the moving car for furniture and building material, and the many couples she had transported to the altar, "for richer or poorer and in sickness and in health." On a few occasions I recall her with the hatch upward, transporting frightened goats tethered to one another, bound for slaughter and baptism in delicious curry. And on any given night when someone took seriously ill within the community and the herbs and bushes were unable to solve the problem, she would be summoned to take them from Moneague to St. Ann's Bay hospital, miles and miles away down through Walker's Wood, Colgate and Fern Gully, to see if by chance any doctors were on duty before morning light.

The interior wiring, which was once underneath the cushions of her seat, now protruded upward with a vengeance to harass and aggravate the derriere of those, including me, who dared to sit. She would snag panty hose daily, thus cutting right into the very core of the measly paycheck at the end of the month. But through it all, she was forgiven and loved, as she remained the only hope for our arrival to the children who awaited and adored our presence in the classroom in Watsonville.

Her driver, affectionately called Mister Feddie, may his soul rest in peace, kept his eyes partially closed as he hummed and whistled along. I know he was accompanied by greater anointing, since he would open his eyes only when he sensed the need to swerve from a threatening tree trunk or some other obstacle, like a loose cow running in his path. We were at his mercy, and prayed incessantly that he remained faithful in the Lord, while he steered this vehicle past Swamp Lake which was renowned for swallowing human beings and buildings alike. The Lake was a manmade piece of landscape which was mined out by the thriving Bauxite Company on the island, leaving in actuality an endless basin for heavy rains and underground water to accumulate. The color of the water was red from the residual Bauxite, and legend had it, that it was as deep as hell. There was an ominous period of silence inside the vehicle each morning while it clunked pass Swamp Lake, and I knew everyone was saying the same prayer for our driver to be in good secular standing. During the evening trips, we seemed more confident about his driving, since school would always dismiss with the prayer: Lighten our darkness, we beseech thee, O Lord; and by thy great mercy defend us from all perils and dangers of this night; for the love of thy only Son, our Savior, Jesus Christ, Amen. We were well covered and protected from the perils which were rumored to lie in the belly of this lake.

Nothing seemed to stand in our way of arriving at Watsonville School, consistently and on time five days per week. We taught diligently, and through our own contributions made the teaching aids necessary to allow our students to learn. We mastered the art of teaching even Science, without expensive or complex teaching aids. Science was in everything we did, so it was easy to find an illustration to explain any scientific concept to the children. It was mere science that allowed us to arrive at the classroom each morning in one piece, since it was gravity that kept our vehicle grounded. Paper planes which we colored and sailed to each other, was our fun way of teaching about gravitational force and the wind. The same sheet of paper would be smoothed out and used for writing in the next lesson. Nothing was wasted.

We knew of the lost cause of relying on the Ministry of Education to help in this endeavor, and so we provided the teaching aids for the children with pleasure—just as those innocent beings shared the produce that their fathers so arduously tilled the soil to bring forth. They caringly turned up to classes with heads of purple yam, pum-pum yam, half-ripe breadfruits, mangoes, and smiles of appreciation just for Teacher.

Dedication and satisfaction in teaching grew more and more insufficient for economic sustenance and educational advancement. But even amid the restlessness, my spirituality was steadfast. There was always an inner voice that whispered in consolation, "Seek ye first the kingdom of God, and all things shall be added unto you." I knew deep down I had sought His kingdom, and so there was no trouble believing the latter part about what good things would follow.

With opportunities to grow seeming better overseas, I pondered the thought of forsaking the greenness of the hills, the blueness of the ocean, and the depths of my personal valleys in pursuit of greener grass. Contemplation grew daily over what I now understand to have been the essence of the words of Anais Nin: "the day came when the risk to remain tight in the bud was more painful than the risk it took to blossom." I eventually decided to leave.

Regarding that moment of decision and the ones immediately leading up to it, I cried uncontrollably for reasons I had been scared to visit emotionally until this moment of truth. Had I known the words of Maxwell's song during this period of decision-making, I would have sung it over and over to myself: "Things I should have said, but I did not say. Things I should have done, but I did not do."

Time wasted trying to breathe life into a dysfunctional relationship. Worrying over insignificant things, which others might perceive to be running away from life's challenges. Being away from my loved ones. The haunting list of guilt went on and on and on.

With all the emotional whirlwind ruffling every fabric of my being, I made so many decisions at this point in my life. Through many experiences as my father's daughter, still too painful and deep-seated to explain, I made the decision at that crucial time to be a tree of many flowers, bearing no fruits. I maintained the courage of my convictions, which were many.

The truth was that I was leaving the life I had come to know for all my years, embarking on that of which I had no knowledge. Going away from those whom I still had so many questions for and with whom so many relationships to strengthen. The ones I truly loved, but I was unsure if they even knew how much. There was no mending of fences via phone cards or sharing emotions for a dollar a minute over phone lines with so much static drowning out the spoken words. There was no turning back. Having said my good-byes, the time was at hand to collect my emotions and press on.

I would miss the ocean the most. It was a place where I had spent many Sunday afternoons alone. Its depth was synonymous with my many thoughts. Its treasures, which were hidden in its soul, were to me the part of my existence no one knew. I admired its beauty and respected the way its spirit could grow angry and then calm again. It appeared during these moments of turmoil that it was abiding to the words I often adhered to, "Peace be still." It always seemed to get angry when the sky got eerie and black. Someone up there was talking to its waves, because after a while of watching, I would see its friendly face again—the face I was so accustomed to gaze into when we spoke. The richness of its turquoise blue color was a symbol of its purity which I admired.

As I took my belongings, one piece at a time, to the waiting vehicle, I couldn't bear to see the tears welling up in the eyes of my stepmom, a loving and caring woman who had nurtured me since the tender age of four, embedding in me all the social graces and proper decorum, which guided my maturity into the well-rounded woman I would eventually become. She was such a stickler for modesty concerning all sartorial matters that any sighting of a color, crease, line, or formation of an undergarment showing through the outer garment would result in a swift return to my bedroom to change.

At the moment of my impending departure, she made one last gesture without saying a word, and it meant the world to me. She reached out, held my hand, and removed a ring she was wearing, one she had cherished with much sentiment ever since she'd owned it. She gently placed it on my finger and helped it over my plump joint, which was two sizes up from her own. The significance of the gesture, the story she told by the look in her eyes, and the symbol of that band encrusted with its amethyst stone made me realize that she knew the meaning of the words "no greater love has no man than this." She gave of herself always. A woman of substance.

Had I gotten the opportunity, I would have made sure that my mother knew I was cherished in the same way she would have cherished me. But time passed, and so did she. I have a feeling, though, that she knew and was content that I had been in phenomenal hands. I have reassured her so many times when I spoke to her through the waves of the ocean.

Two

Tough

The decision to immigrate was one that I met with mixed emotions: guilt from a gut-wrenching recreant feeling, and also one of deserting my obligation to give back, if only to those children whom I had the initial pleasure of teaching.

I comforted myself or justified my action with the words of Robert Jordan, which reminded me that "the oak fought the wind and was broken. The willow bent when it must and survived." I had bent. I was quite familiar with the flexibility and strength of the willow, despite its stark difference in size and stature in comparison to the unmovable oak. The wind could be unpredictable and a force of nature to be reckoned with. I knew at times it was capable of blowing one right off his or her footing.

But through it all, I sealed my decision with a personal promise that if Jordan was right as far as survival, then I would ensure that others would benefit from not only my tales of survival, but from some tangible good learned from my personal sacrifice.

I started my life in America with simple intentions. The first was to look up those who had come before me, and hear from them how they had unlocked this giant door and made good on the dream. This proved to be a challenge, as there was no Facebook at the time. Reconnecting with friends and old schoolmates meant waiting on happenstance. Oftentimes I would run into an old acquaintance who would know a relative of the person with whom I was trying to reconnect. Telephone numbers would be exchanged and time would drag on for months before the number would reach its desired destination. Then suddenly the long lost friend would appear on the line, only to bring some shocking news of how they had already fallen on hard times and needed advice from me (the newcomer). I recall with much sadness, one night after going through multiple people to get a telephone number for an old friend and schoolmate that had come to America not too long before I had arrived, I finally found a mutual friend who knew both her telephone number and her address. We were from the same tiny close-knit community in paradise, and everyone there thought we shared strikingly similar physical characteristics, mannerisms and taste in dress. I knew she must have had some stories to tell since her arrival, and desperately needed to hear from her what was going on. This mutual friend agreed to drive me in the general vicinity of my friend's address, so that after we got over the initial reunion via telephone, we could surprisingly meet in less than a few minutes outside her building.

I called her telephone number. Excitement was mounting as it rang. A man picked up the telephone and after introducing myself he told me he was her father. There was a feeling of sadness coming from his end of the telephone. Then he managed to let out a quiet sigh of, "aah." My initial reaction was a question which I came up with, just to fill the moment of silence. She is not at home? I knew there was more to his sigh and sadness, but at the time, that was the only thing I could think of asking. He calmly told me my friend (his daughter), had been rushed to the hospital and had passed away. I was in complete shock, devastation and awe. Just like the many times in my youth when I had tried to compare the resemblance which the people in paradise saw in both of us, I began to immediately see myself in her place. People in paradise often described this sad, unfortunate and devastating type of situation as, "leaving your country in good health and returning in a box." To this day, I often wonder what would Pat have been doing now? I know it would have been something great because heaven has sure received an Angel.

After many disappointments and delays in reconnecting with friends, my next intention was to follow the advice of Confucius. But my intentions were complicated by reality and realizations. First, the bitterness of winter brought on nostalgia. Then, the longing for the hot summer sun, complemented by the soothing island breeze and turquoise beaches, made me soon seize every opportunity from my penny jar in order to board our beloved Air Jamaica, which we affectionately called our "lovebird," for frequent visits back to paradise. Air Jamaica was like no other airline, as it felt like you were on a bus trip whenever you flew on this lovebird. Passengers from paradise would just board the aircraft and sit wherever the heck they felt like sitting. If you were a little late for takeoff, you just looked around for an empty seat. If none was available, you would be escorted off the plane by the friendly flight attendant who would explain that the flight was simply overbooked. It was no problem at all for Air Jamaica to have two hundred seats on the aircraft and sell five hundred tickets. Also, the date of departure was always an estimate. It was never advisable to plan anything important around this date. Upon arrival at the airport ticket counter for a morning flight, it could result in the ticket attendant directing you to choose another morning. The thing with Air Jamaica, why we loved it so much, was that we could bring anything on board, no problem at all. Sometimes the aircraft would be on the tarmac for hours, due to some passenger insisting on boarding with everything and the kitchen sink in tow. On one occasion when a flight I was being checked in for, had clearly been overbooked, the ticket agent announced that passengers in line would not be able to check on any excess boxes or luggage regardless of their ability to pay for them. Whenever Air Jamaica refused money, I was always deeply concerned as to whether the aircraft could remain in the sky, as this implied that the plane was already heavily laden. However, this gentleman who was behind me in line with a box almost as tall as he was, had no concern whatsoever for the announcement. He quickly asked a rhetorical question, "Wha shi say?" while switching his head rapidly from side to side. He then busted the box open and out of it emerged a decorated five foot white Christmas Tree which he insisted on checking on, now that he had gotten rid of the problem- the box. The agent had a warm time explaining to this gentleman why it was, that he could not check on his snowy white artificial tree destined for Jamaica, when he clearly had no box and a tree was not considered luggage. Regardless of everything, we loved Air Jamaica. It didn't land on time, but it always landed safely, sometimes with the luggage compartment empty.

It wasn't long before occasional visits turned into expensive frequent-flying bouts, and my financial ability to sustain them was in dire straits. This is the period of time in life when we hear the haunting voices of the older folks saying, "Settle down." Usually when we first begin to hear these words from whomever our mentors were, we would shrug them off as hindrances which stood in the way of our fun. But at this time in my life, nostalgia or not, these words were my warning to begin a stable and orderly existence, by coming to grips with the decision I had voluntarily made. I had to pull up my socks and indeed settle down.

I guess every immigrant, or most of us, go through this process of adaptation. Throughout this phase, the lyrics of Admiral Bailey's hit song "No Way No Better than

Yard" resonated constantly in my head, tormented me in my dreams, and chased me incessantly to nightclubs to hear some of my other favorites at that poignant time in my life. Those days when nostalgia set in like a plague and Reggae artists did roll call in the club, all I had to do was shake the doom and gloom and join the revellers on the dance floor, and dance the night away. Beres Hammond would wind things down with one of those deep love songs, and for those who didn't have a special someone, or a boops for that matter, Super Cat would show them one with "See Boops Deh." While they were looking for boops, I would hurry home in the wee hours of the morning to catch a few hours of sleep for wherever I was destined to go the next day for a job, which the temp agency was dreaming up for me.

These jobs varied from place to distant places and required diverse skills, which these temp agencies did not care much if I possessed. Their main goal was to have someone show-up, as they had promised their clients they would do. At times I would show-up with the expectation of providing elderly care, and would be redirected to de-flea the dogs and bedding, and shampoo the cats just in case they too were infected. Then off to the laundry mat where I would scan the Classified section in the newspaper while the machines spun and tumbled with loads and loads of clothes, beddings and such the like. Only after then, would the elderly care take place.

I would then check in with the agency representative to see if she had concocted any more jobs for me. Usually hoping that my next location would be nearby. But hope seemed as if it had abandoned me, and I was like that scorned girlfriend who would cling to a looser despite being let down time and time again. I guess like me, she felt confident that this time around would be his last time letting her down. The representative would answer the telephone, telling me how much the last client had loved me and that I was good with the animals. She would try to get me to go back there next week, but in the meantime, she had a very easy job just across the Whitestone Bridge in Queens. The client just needed help with a few things, as she was unable to get around much without the aid of her motorized chair. So hope was dashed in terms of the distance between the two jobs, as I was leaving from one borough to the next. But the part relating to the "few things" was what I was now depending on hope to help me with. After dealing with these representatives for a while, I realized that they tried very hard not to elaborate on herculean tasks, and will even down-play the magnitude of the clients' requests, just to win a client over.

Most people were heading home from work, but I was heading to my second engagement for the day, clear across the East River, to do "a few things." One of the main things with "settling down" was that you had to be flexible, skip being picky and avoid turning down jobs. Otherwise, the agencies would not call whenever temp jobs became available. After getting over the initial hurdle of locating one Queens's residence by using the barrage of numbers and dashes in the street address, I am greeted at the door by the client. We sit to discuss the few things which she had hoped would have been accomplished earlier on during the day. Nightfall appeared to be a bit problematic for her. Something about this was not going as good as I had hoped. Despite being anxious to hear the details, it would have been impolite to rush the client. Eventually, after hearing about forty years of her life's story which was memorialized with various gifts and collectibles stacked inside her basement, she arrived at the specifics about the service she had requested of the agency. Transferring the contents of the basement to her detached garage, which was already busting at the seams. Access to the basement was via a narrow staircase which was highly unstable, as the steps had become loose, squeaky and lopsided over the years. The path between the garage and the basement-exit was overgrown with weeds, and by her own account, raccoons had found their way inside the garage, and were using it as a breeding ground for their family.

Still unsure as to how I would have broken the news to my client, that this was way beyond the scope of what I had imagined to be a few things, I descended the basement staircase while she waited at the top for my return. I picked up the nearest item to the foot of the stairs, from the mountain of things which were visible. It was an old floor lamp, without the shade, which proved challenging to maneuver with one hand going up the stairs. I needed to keep my other hand free, not only for balance but for cobweb defense as well.

The lamp and the memories attached to it, were enough to take us into dusk, giving me the opportunity to explain that the agency would be in touch for future scheduling. The agency representative reluctantly saw my point that a moving company; a carpenter, a wild-life animal catcher and a landscaper were all needed, and not an elderly care aid as was first imagined.

I continued to rely on the Classifieds, and on hope that the temp agencies would in the meantime be merciful in their job placement strategies. I took constant comfort seeing and hearing people from different countries and walks of life speaking different languages as they went about their businesses day after day, by means of travel both underground and aboveground—literally and figuratively. In the literal sense, I was taken straight out of my element, as paradise had not offered me any preparative experiences in the navigation of subway lines, alphabetically or numerically labeled, running through darkness from one screeching stop to another.

And even stranger was the fact that people were packed in these train cars literally standing over those who were lucky to find a seat and not saying a single solitary word to one another, not even "Good Morning," as they stretched their armpits over the heads of those below. Where did they find spaces to stare into in a vehicle where every halting stop landed you on top of another person? But no one made eye contact, so obviously there was an art in finding distance and personal space in a crammed subway car. More frightening to me was the way people would move slightly away from others who dared to lose their balance when the tram jolted. To me, this was a sure sign that falling in this big city was inevitable. Being sure that you are tough enough to get up was the only requirement for survival along the journey.

The subways at that time as artistic as they were, covered in graffiti, they also marked the absence of chivalry, which was immediately noticed by me, emigrating from an island previously ruled by the British. Moral and social codes that included relinquishing your seat for the elderly or for those nearing labor were embedded in people in my native land by the principles that we were taught at an early age. But among straphangers (I later learned that subway riders were called that, because of the looped leatherette strap that we held on to, in order to prevent a fall), no one exercised chivalry. Pregnant women, even those bearing quadruplets, with their navels protruding through their clothing, were seemingly left to stand and hold on to the straps above their heads; the man below them was intensely reading the *New York Times*, which he could not fully open, as its pages were huge and her stomach was in the way. So rather than get up and offer his seat, this wretched man would fold the pages of the *Times* in quarters, like a book, and block the sight of this humongous belly standing over him. This was simply not permitted in paradise. The pregnant and the elderly received carte blanche from anyone with whom they came into contact. Everyone who identified with these two groups had one of two titles, "Mommy" or "Daddy." So in any situation (not subway cars, though, because we did not have those in our mountains) where a seat was needed, the able would rise and say, "Come, Mommy (or Come, Daddy), have a seat." It was as simple as that. Sometimes three or four volunteers would jump up saying, "Come tek dis one," and Mommy or Daddy would have a choice as to where to sit. Here it was a bit more complicated, and some were taking extra steps to conceal the obvious reasons to be kind. Like making origami out of the *Times*.

Another issue was that the method of payment for a trip via the subway when I arrived, devised by some genius, was the token. It was a circular coin, gold in color, of no particular monetary denomination. The process of obtaining same was to go to a glass-enclosed, six-by-nine-foot box with a human being locked up like Houdini and sweating profusely, equipped with a distorting microphone. The box had a space under the glass with a metal tray, in which the token would be slid out to the potential rider only after the one-dollar bill was snatched up by the person inside said glass box. This person in the glass case seemed to be in the same unfriendly mood every day. The only pride exhibited was to waste the rider's time in asking over and over what was needed, just when the train was rolling into the station. All the rider ever wanted was a damn token; after all, that was the only item being sold. So I missed the point of the echoing microphone and the repeated questions, which would eventually result in missing the train that would only stop for a minute in the station. This unfriendly delay seemed intentional. Someone had to be punished for someone else's enclosure in a glass box.

On very rare occasions when it became necessary to ask directions as to what alphabetical or numerical subway line to take to a desired destination, the token would hit the metal slot underneath the glass, followed by a cold, distorted response that sounded like "take the F line to the U, change to the C, and keep going all the way to the last stop." Needless to say, traveling underground was like a "Coming to America" boot camp. But something about the existence of the trains made everything and everywhere seem reachable. There were no racial, economic, or social lines of separation among the riders. Everyone took it. Every country was represented, just like in the Olympics.

One obvious note among the various groups of riders was that the foreigners, traveling with one another each day, were divided into three distinctive subsets, or permutations like my sagacious elementary schoolteacher would say. I was wondering when I would be able to apply that little "set and subset" phenomenon of permutations, which was such a pain to learn in primary school.

Mrs. Tait would drive that point home with the leather strap at the ready for those who harbored any limitations in mastering mathematical theories. And again, the strap worked out just fine. No obvious signs of childhood trauma have lingered. So fast-forward to real-life lessons, where the concept is being put to use in the subway clear across the ocean.

Those little circles overlapping one another in the Venn diagram on the chalkboard meant something. They intersected. Back then the mere size of that word made everything seem impossible to learn. It is all clear now, though, that these sets of foreigners had something in common that linked them, and yet they had some other things that were different. I drew the three circles overlapping one another one day on the subway and began to fill in the commonalities and the differences. Thanks to the strap.

One subset possessed the all-purpose document, which was believed to lead all immigrants to the doors of opportunity, behind which the American dream was shuttered. This document had long been known and recognized by us, as a people, as the "papers," although it was legally named the Resident Alien Green Card, emblazoned with a carefully prepared A-number lest the holder forget who he or she was. In its legal definition, we found that the word "alien" was associated with extra-terrestrial beings. Looking even deeper, we found that it meant, "an outsider, or one who doesn't belong." And now my feelings erupted into vexation at the realization of how welcome I was in a land where I truly belonged, to suddenly be categorized otherwise by the mere designation of an A-number.

But out of self-affirmation and steadfast determination to fiercely protect my dignity, I decided to settle with a meaning that surfaced now and then: "non-citizen resident of a country." Aha! So that was who the millions of foreigners in subset A were. My grand-mother Lydia, affectionately called Mammie, a very wise woman of few words, often said, "It's not what you are called that matters, but it's what you choose to answer to." Mammie was not really a stickler for the leather strap per se, though she would sometimes sur-prise us with the back of her hand, if the need arose. I never knew any woman as powerful as Mammie. She ruled over the entire Bell family, whether you lived in England, America, or Jamaica. And she did it right from a stool she sat on inside of her shop, in the center of Hope Bay town in Portland. Through Mammie, I wasn't going to let the alien name-calling affect me in any shape or form.

Anyway, as time passed and the members of this sub-set qualifies to become citizens, they acquired the actual key, it is said, to unlock the dream door and even par-ticipate in the democratic process, subset B. Their ability to cast a vote was undoubtedly one of the most valuable civic privileges and was now a duty of being a member of subset B.

I later realized how many in subset A were so dis-traught when they were excluded from helping to elect the forty-fourth president of the United States of America. They truly understood the meaning of "alien" at that time, even though they were all mandatorily quali-fied to participate in the IRS process or in the protection of the freedoms of the United States of America in any armed service that they chose to join.

But I'll pause to provide some consolation merely out of empathy for this same permutation, that many unwarranted attempts were made to include the president himself in subset A. There was the question of the birth certificate not being authentic, which would bring into speculation his inclusion in "B" and ultimately his qualification to be number forty-four.

All politics aside, when efforts to disqualify us on our record or our ambitiousness seemed to fail, the next point of attack was oftentimes the place from whence we came. But in case there is still one immigrant left who has not yet experienced this type of repression, be patient. You will.

Subset C, lest we forget, were the hardest workers, who, by the way, were forbidden to work without the qualifying documents and were classified one step lower than the aliens. They were illegal aliens. As if it were not demeaning enough to be an alien, insult had just been added to fury by the preceding adjective.

That's another thing— "the power of the adjective"— that the third grade teacher tried to reinforce, to which I did not pay much attention. I'll admit to and blame that lack of attention now on the many bags of Cheez Doodles and banana chips, which I hid and passed to others under the desks as sentence structure was being taught. The importance of the adjective and its descriptive nature in building or demolishing what it precedes. Its power over subset C said, "Don't even think about giving your real name if you are asked, and at the sight of the police or any type of excitement that involves the law, get the hell out of Dodge!"

Subset C, it seemed, always had a fear that often bordered on paranoia for any being wearing a white shirt. These were the men presumed to be from the wretched INS, which later changed its name to ICE. The latter reflected a frigid tolerance for the people in question, always hounding them in their sleep and on the trains to and from the jobs that they were forbidden to hold. Members of subset C even spoke in parables on the telephone for fear these men might be listening. It's illogical to think of a government so equipped to pay millions of eavesdroppers to catch subset C on the telephone. But oh no, you couldn't tell them anything, as it remained a sure illusion they were being watched, followed, and listened to night and day. No papers, no convincing. I can just imagine them saying, "I told you so," when Wiki began leaking and the disloyal Snowden claimed to have confirmed their worst fears. I strongly doubt that any government in the free world is interested in its citizens talking about their grocery lists and other minor details of their personal lives, which they share and LOL with one another before hanging up.

Once the Classifieds paid off and hope joined forces with faith, I bade the temp agencies good-bye. For seven years I would ride the subway, enduring the heat of the number two and the number five trains with my fellow straphangers, holding on for dear life with one hand and protecting the valuables in my pocketbook with the other. Most of all in my subway experiences, I dreaded the way the fire would gash from the metal rubbing the tracks on the passing trains, and then the electricity inside the car would temporarily flicker and go out. No one warned me against this, and my initial experience of it proved I was not emotionally prepared. Had I experienced this a few years later on, I would have been sure that someone from inside a cave had something to do with it.

It was during frightening experiences such as these that I missed paradise the most. For our natives took pride in warning one another against impending or perceived dangers. A simple episode of flashing lights anywhere in paradise would have warranted the shouts of, "Fire! Fire!" A stampede would have broken out, and anyone trampled would have been taken care of by his or her fellow passengers, as the one ambulance that would have arrived would have been directed to the very seriously mauled with extreme clout in the community. But here, no one flinched, and after many occurrences of these incidences of sparks followed by darkness, I eventually grew accustomed to it.

Arrival at my new cubicle each morning was a staunch reminder of how small paradise was in comparison to the dreamland, and yet how limited space seemed here for the existence of humankind. Eight hours in a cubicle. Even the word itself, if researched, does not present to be a place for human beings. But not only was it my kennel for the day, but it housed my computer, reference books, telephone, and my drawers. The interior of the box was carpeted, making it easy to hang memos with thumbtacks for a quick read. Memos were distributed so frequently that ironically there were memos advising that we would soon be receiving a memo of a new procedure or rate changes for a certain product.

There was warning of a high level of productivity that was expected of me, in order to maintain my employment status with this Telephone Company which was dominating the industry at the time. Such a level was measured by the number of new telephone lines sold and the products and services sold to existing customers. The company was so strict about selling these darn telephone calling features that if a customer called about a line having no dial tone, we had to apologize and then sucker the customer into buying something. Imagine, you're not able to use your telephone, and someone tries to get you to buy call waiting. Then we were required to get subscribers to relinquish their rotary-wheel dial telephones, the ones where you stuck one finger in the dial hole and turned the wheel all the way around. These were to be replaced with touch-tone push-button telephone sets—for a price, of course.

Sometimes I would tell them how I had arthritis and the touch-tone push button was a blessing, so they should try it free for thirty days. Sucker. Sold. Make no mistake: if they didn't call back to cancel the thirty-day free trial, I was following up to attach a bill onto their original monthly commitment. No callback meant that they liked it, and the company couldn't be happier.

There was the general understanding that each of the calls I answered was being monitored to ensure quality service to the public. I often wondered why the monitors did not come out of their hiding places and answer some of the damn phone lines that were ringing. This to me would have provided even faster and better service to the members of the public. However, I dared not waste time to utter a word about it, causing the public to wait on eternal hold on the lines, for one of my fellow cubiconians to say on my behalf, "Hope I've provided you with excellent service today." All hell would rain asunder if those words were not uttered before ending one call and greeting the holding public on the other.

The most tedious time of the year was during the ending of the summer, when college students from Maine, Arkansas, and never-never land trickled to the Big Apple to attend college in September. They demanded telephone service in their dorm rooms and demanded the same to be connected at the touch of a switch. In addition, they must get a dedicated line for their modem and one for their fax. Otherwise their homework and projects could not be completed. By the way, I still had a typewriter at home, which was performing just fine. This miracle that they ordered of the alien in the cubicle must take place within twenty-four hours. I often wondered during the two seconds before the next call if this whining little brat on the phone knew I was stuck inside a two-by-four carpeted box with nowhere to go.

My immediate supervisor was a darling of a lady, standing about five feet ten inches, with silky blond hair, a stickler for cubiconians to answer on the first half ring.

She exhibited no reservation in entering my tiny little space to bring my attention to someone's phone service that I had prevented from going on because of some code I had neglected to input into the computer. Because of my error, the computer had failed to send the proper signal over fiber-optic cables, and thus the little brat's boyfriend could not call to check up on her in the Big Apple. Having my supervisor, or anyone for that matter, share my space was complete torture. More than that, though, was the task of getting accustomed to the codes that were supposed to be entered to activate the telephone lines. Why on earth couldn't the company have ensured that telephone connections be processed in plain English and not binary codes? If it had done that in the interest of the public in the first place, I would not have forgotten to add some stupid equation, which resulted in a dissatisfied customer and which could potentially result in me having no job. But for the most part, my performance was exemplary, and my supervisor was fair, except when she was bent on sharing my working space.

The issue of limited space in a place known for its vast richness and enormity wasn't the only realization that was stunning in the eyes of this immigrant. During the orientation for the job, I discovered that employees were entitled to one initial week of vacation, gradually climbing to four weeks per year upon attaining five consecutive years of service. There was no mention of a "leave," which is a period of several months away from work, separate from a vacation. It comes in two fashions back in paradise— "long leave" and "short leave," both are paid time off designed to rejuvenate the human body and mind. Employees in all sectors in paradise when utilizing their accumulated time or "time on the books" as we so often call it, can choose to take that time off in increments of a few weeks or extended months at a time. For instance, teachers accumulate four months after four years of service, separate from their summer holidays. If they choose not to take the time off, then it increases to eight weeks after eight years of service, and so on. But not here in America, not even a siesta in the afternoons like in Spain. Work, work, and more work.

Growing competition in the world of technology was rapidly mounting in the late 1980s, and telephone companies were popping up everywhere, even in basements of unsuspecting buildings, with the founders charging a dollar a minute for a recording of some voice breathing seductively on the other end. Unemployed tricksters were even sitting in their apartments answering phone lines pretending to be clairvoyants, telling callers that they were destined for high-paying jobs, rich husbands, and the like, while charging these callers nine ninety-nine a minute for bogus fortunetelling. There were handsets coming out that could tell the phone line to dial a number when you just said the name of whom you were trying to reach. You could block the number of the person from whom you couldn't stand to hear. And star sixty-nine was a big trend for those who wanted to find out who was harassing them. Or star sixty-seven, for the harasser to maintain anonymity. Forget call-waiting, damn! You could turn that off and talk for hours, running your bill up so you wouldn't even be disturbed by the beep.

It was a period of time when people were gradually ceasing to carry their car radios around in their hand, out of fear the car would be broken into. Cellular telephones weighed about ten pounds and were as bulky as a pair of size ten Timberlands. They mainly came in beige, with a thick antenna, and did not work in most places. But when you were hauling one around, you were looked at twice—either as a legitimate businessperson, a rich individual, or a dealer of pharmaceuticals. The latter would also have a few beepers on their belts, in case the telephone signal did not work at a time when their clients wanted a delivery.

My company changed its name during this period of technological advancement and customer hoodwinking, perhaps to mislead the public that it was so concerned about, into believing that they were new and different. Those unsuspecting subscribers would not even realize they were getting the same level of service under a different name and at a higher fee.

It took me a while to get used to answering my calls with the new name, and every time I misstated the company's new name, by saying, "New York Telephone, oh, excuse me …." I had to be squashed by my supervisor and be reminded that I was being warned for the last time that in my greeting to the public, there was to be no mention of the old name of the telephone company. I had to be cognizant of the fact that the Public Service Commission would run test calls from time to time and would levy heavy fines due to any mistakes made to misinform the public. That old name was associated with losing profits and poor service and deceptive practices. Maybe because we were conveniently forgetting to call customers back to remind them to return their thirty-day free-trial touch-tone telephone sets.

I was determined not to deceive my customers anymore. So each morning I made an effort to repeat the new name of the company over and over on the subway, amid gashing fire on the tracks and occasional darkness in the subway cars. Then I would arrive, confident that I had rehearsed the proper codes for the computer to perform its fiber-optic connections, and that I had the name of the company down pat. I adjusted my headset, pulled the thin microphone with the black sponge bud along my jaw, and answered my first call.

As always, I was very delighted to assist the caller in whatever matters of telephone service or dedicated computer line service that was required. "How can I provide you with excellent service today?" There was a distinct voice on the other end, bearing an accent that I had no difficulty identifying. It was similar to my own, thick and straight out of paradise. After a few questions, it was clear this was a person with a very simple request. Only a mere dial tone was needed—no extras and no complicated trimmings such as call forwarding, speed dialing, three-way calling, or voice dialing. Hell! This caller did not even grasp the fact that phones started to dial a number if you said "Boo" into the mouthpiece.

She was pleasant and very respectful; she persisted in addressing me as ma'am throughout our conversation. I wondered here and there to what subset she belonged, but knew that truth would be revealed soon enough. In fact, it was time for me to acquire credit information that would attest to her ability to meet her monthly financial obligations for the dial tone. I read the credit disclaimer regarding prospective subscribers providing false credit information and the risk of prosecution. Um! I detected deep breathing from the other end of the line. That disclaimer had a way of creating the same reaction as when a person hears the Miranda warning being recited to him or her. Something about it tells you, you could be in deep trouble. I asked for a valid social security number or tax identification number. Judging from the long pause, punctuated by several agonal gasps, it became evident that the inference of taxes was a problem, and that a newly purchased social security number was about to be given to me. Furthermore, it was clear that the new owner of this social was being careful that it was configured with nine digits and no more.

I waited with patience and understanding as I drew my three little overlapping circles on my notepad. I inputted the nine numbers I received from the caller into the computer and waited for Equifax, Transunion, and Experian to kick back their respective responses simultaneously—while recalling another realization that back then in paradise, there was no credit bureau, and people were judged for the approval of credit based on factors such as political affiliation, royal lineage, existing wealth, agricultural prowess from produce such as that which was being legalized in the United States today, and also based on other factors still difficult to decipher. My computer screen went dark for a quick second, and then it lit up again, showing responses from Equifax, Transunion, and Experian, which all said, "Social Security number expired; please verify the number and reenter it."

I thought about asking my caller to repeat the number, but was concerned that such a request could potentially trigger any underlying coronary medical conditions she might have. I decided to blame myself for perhaps not hearing her clearly and asked if she would be so kind as to repeat it since I might have written it down incorrectly. She quickly obliged and recited it once more, perhaps feeling a bit more empowered that I was capable of admitting to a mistake. The numbers were the same ones I had previously typed, and hence the credit responses were correct.

This was the first indication that not only was my caller deceased, according to her Social Security number, but she was definitely a ghost in subset C. I immediately informed her, as per protocol and possible monitoring, that due to a discrepancy with the credit bureaus regarding the status of the social, I was recommending that she respond in person to a walk-in telephone center with various pieces of identification and a lease for the place in which she was requesting telephone service. I sounded silly to myself, asking that a ghost, or "jumbie" according to the dialect, should respond in person.

Disappointment was evident on her part, and I couldn't decipher my own feelings. She wanted to know, just before she hung up, what was meant by discrepancy. Did she really want me to lay it on the line? Was she aware that the men wearing the white shirts listened to everything? Well, as soon as I informed her she was no longer among the living and would not need a telephone in that case, she said "all right, all right den," and disconnected from me. I suspected she ran off to try to locate the seller of the social. There would be no resolution for her, as both buyer and seller would have been scared to go to the men in blue to file a complaint.

I took many such calls with varying degrees of discrepancy, where names and socials did not coincide, and dead people from many different countries were on the other end of the telephone. And many socials belonged to newborns, who can't even talk to be in need of a telephone in the first place. Other callers, when told of the discrepancy, suddenly "no speaky English, y no comprehende nada." Then there were those immigrants who harbored certain superstitions toward particular numbers, and as soon as I assigned them a telephone number that contained the digit "four," they would tell me, "naah, can't take evil numba, need different numba." After being informed that there would be a monthly fee for choosing one's own telephone number, they would ask me, "how mosh?" Every day there was a lesson, however small, on

cultural diversity, organizational deception, and technological advancement.

Toward the ending of the 1980s we staged a long
strike, in opposition to a new contract that the union
rejected. Employees were issued red T-shirts, which we
donned to walk the picket line in protest. During the
strike, it dawned on me how powerful unions were here,
in comparison to those in paradise. The strike lasted for
months, and each time the company presented an offer,
the union would reject it, until an arbitrator was called
in. Bills began to pile up as the union paid the mortgage
or rent of employees plus ten dollars per hour for time
spent picketing. No credit card bills and no food money.
I would march in a circle all day, every day, rejecting
offers left and right, despite the fact that I was broke and
hungry.

Anyone from paradise will explain that we are a people who cannot remain unemployed for too long of a
period. Even within a twenty-four-hour period, it is not
uncommon for us to work a twelve-hour shift and two
six-hour shifts, all at different places. We use our lunch
break to travel between jobs, so we are never late. Sleep
usually takes place during the travel time. Television
shows such as the hilarious, "Living Color," portrayed us
as workaholics with four different types of jobs running
simultaneously. One of my cousins who had arrived here
before I did, had called me one day to explain that she
was seeking a second job. I knew she worked seven days
per week, and so I enquired of her if she intended to
drop a day or two from her current job. She politely told

me, that she intended to work this new job on the eighth day of the week.

So, as the strike progressed and being the Jamigrant that I am, I picketed during the daytime and secured a night job at a doctor's answering service. This gig was so convenient. No one entered the facility at night, so I could wear my pink sponge rollers and bed slippers and forego the makeup while I answered the telephones. Doctors would leave varying instructions regarding which patients they could be disturbed for and which ones I should inform that they were in surgery. Many of the patients on the could-be list were professional athletes and people with clout. Sometimes I felt guilty telling the same hypochondriac patient on the do-not-disturb list over and over that Dr. Steinfell was in surgery and could not come to the telephone at the moment. Sometimes Dr. Steinfell said he would be away with Mrs. Steinfell overnight and did not wish to be disturbed. Then about half past four in the morning, when I was trying to get some sleep to go picket for my ten dollars, Mrs. Steinfell would call in the middle of the night. I would tell her he was in an emergency surgery. Then I would call him on his emergency pager to forewarn him before he got home the next day. Dr. Steinfell was always in emergency surgery at least three times per month, though it was impossible to tell if he was working on the same patient or different ones. He would stop by to drop off his check for the service sometimes and would hand me a little envelope for the great work I was doing in making sure his surgical procedures went on without a hitch.

This little gig was interesting, to say the least, and enough to cover the other bills that the union did not help with. At least it made me laugh. After arbitration, a reasonable settlement was reached, and normalcy resumed at my company. I didn't have to deceive Mrs. Steinfell anymore, and so I asked for forgiveness and went back to my regular job.

After a while, I decided to break the monotony of the job by examining the many benefits that the company offered. I tapped into the tuition reimbursement program, a welcome opportunity that I had not yet enjoyed in paradise, traded my teachers' college credits, and reexamined the status of my progress toward the attainment of the dream.

The choice of college campus reminded me of my alma mater back in paradise. It was secluded away from the hustle and bustle of Broadway, with its high architectural ceilings and well-manicured lawns on which to lie, study, meditate, and oftentimes sleep. The Tapanzee and its body of water blanketed the hill on which the institution nestled. Not far away, the Rockefellers' estate stood, as a sprawling reminder that they too, as German immigrants, had surpassed the financial threshold of the dream. A calm and serene campus. Just what I needed after the subway rides, the fiery train tracks, and the many parties that ended at four in the mornings in a city that never slept. The most comforting fact was that the tuition was covered by my generous company, which ironically did not give its employees any relief from their confined working spaces.

Three

CIVIC PRIDE

The energy in the city and on Broadway, where I worked, was great, especially on Fridays after work. It was a place that embraced life and livelihood twenty-four seven. But for some reason, my mobility and aspirations as far as work seemed cramped, both professionally and physically. I needed more, and I needed a change. This seems to be the mantra of the resourceful immigrant. Especially those who manage to maneuver all the cares of life plus some extras, with minimal sleep. Quickies were the order of the day. A quick lunch, a quick dinner, and a quick whatever else was needful. So this feeling of emptiness was an over-all desire to slow down the pace in terms of whatever was causing these quickies and spend more meaningful time collectively on professional and social existence.

I pondered a career designed to bolster civic pride. After all, anything is possible when we follow our dream. I often admired the words of the thirty-fifth president of the United States in his inaugural address: "...the rights of man come not from the generosity of the state, but from the hand of God...And so, my fellow Americans: ask not what your country can do for you—ask what you can do for your country. My fellow citizens of the world: ask not what America will do for you, but what together we can do for the freedom of man."

My father was not thrilled at my career decision of joining law enforcement. Perhaps due to the dangers inherent in it, and more so, after he was confronted with the fact that I was putting his chosen profession for me aside. Neither of us knew then that I would again return to teaching someday.

After all, I had pledged allegiance to the flag, and civil service was definitely a way to demonstrate that I really meant it. Besides, I had hoped to show the same patriotism to the black, green and gold in paradise, with or without my father's blessings, but at five feet three inches, my patriotism seemed short and insufficient according to the guidelines for admission to the Police Academy back in paradise. Ironically, shortly after my swearing-in ceremony here, I received a lovely letter of commendation from the sitting Jamaican ambassador, Dr. Richard L. Bernal. It was mailed directly from The Embassy of Jamaica to the United States in Washington, DC, and bore the proud seal of paradise, emblazoned with the words, "Out of many, one people." It thanked me overwhelmingly for upholding the country's name overseas and encouraged me to strive to fly the Jamaican flag high so everyone could see it and we could all be proud.

The letter read thusly:

EMBASSY OF JAMAICA
1520 NEW HAMPSHIRE AVE, N.W.
WASHINGTON. D.C. 20036
TELEPHONE. (202)

February 28, 1995

Ms. Marie Bell
Mount Vernon Police Department
1 Roosevelt Square N
Mount Vernon, New York 10550

Dear Ms. Bell:

Please accept my heartiest congratulations in making history by becoming the first Jamaican-born female to be sworn in as a Probationary Police Officer in the Mount Vernon Police Force.

I wish you continued success as you strive to uphold the law and to fly our flag high in the Police Department.

Yours sincerely,

Dr. Richard L. Bernal
Ambassador

For the discerning eye, the document begins with the Jamaican national symbol, the coat of arms, which exudes the motto, "Out of many, one people"—expressing the collective servitude of the people and the unity of the different cultural minorities on the island nation. A clearer depiction of this powerful symbol has been legibly magnified:

His Excellency was not aware that the height requirement in the Jamaica Constabulary Force was still at a level which prevented its qualified patriots from bringing the same level of distinction to their own country. It was indeed an honor to have received his blessing and recognition, while deep down I harbored the hope, that such unnecessary rules which stifled employment back in paradise would be given some attention as well.

Newspaper articles followed the ambassador's acknowledgment, and a few friends called straight from paradise to alert me to the fact that the local radio and television station had delivered the news on the island. My humility to be appreciative has never been compromised by any rejection I experienced then by the JCF or later by anyone who had not given me a job I was qualified for, simply because of some physical characteristic that I possessed. For that matter, I still preserve a copy of the letter and the newspaper clippings to this day.

Come to think of it, the Jamaica Telephone Company, JTC, had rejected me too, on the grounds that I had a lisp that would be unpleasant to callers needing directory assistance. There can be no greater rejection felt in life than one due to a physical characteristic created by God himself.

But then this telephone company here made no mention of it before stuffing me in their cubicle to expeditiously serve the public. Two times I was rejected to serve in paradise and fulfill my duties to the general public. Neither of the rejections was due to anything under my control. Both had everything to do with the way I was born. I often wondered how many others wound up leaving paradise because of rejection they had encountered in the workforce.

Ironically the land of the free and the home of the brave has the exact motto, "E Pluribus Unum," meaning "out of many, one," symbolized on the breast of the eagle on the great seal. What a stark similarity in nations with such seemingly vast differences!

It seemed that a higher power had made that similarity possible, so I became more convinced and encouraged, despite all obstacles, to soar. It is not uncommon in the life of an immigrant to  go through a period of reflection and comparison, in which we search for the reason why we could not accomplish this or that in our native land. Sometimes the reasons are clear and somewhat understandable. Sometimes the reasons are unfair and can either make you or break you. Either way, we must soar like an eagle and be prepared to land like a hawk.

One day while fixing my emotional wings to take off in flight, I drove to my usual place of nearby solace, Glen Island. A quick drive took me to this one hundred-plus acres park, pristinely floating on Long Island Sound. I parked my car, donned my sunglasses, and stared at the seagulls landing on the calm, silver body of water. I dismissed the temptation to make any comparison of the waters or the beach with those in paradise.

Here it was spectacular in its own right, but there was no comparison. I had my usual conversation with the tiny waves, and they whispered back and gently swept my mind to its usual place of solace. I took one brisk lap along the pedestrian walkway, which meandered around the park, not straying far from the water's edge, lest I would miss a subtle splash of advice or caution. I thought of the people who placed messages and notes in bottles and sent them off to sea, hoping that one day their thoughts would float on life's shore. I knew deep down in my soul that my whispers would ride the waves and reach somewhere far as well. The waves rolled gently toward me, and they were listening intently. Ours signified a pure relationship forged in mutual trust, which was built long ago on the shores of paradise. A man and a little boy stood with fishing rods extended in the water, waiting patiently for a tug. I peeked inquisitively inside the bucket and saw that it was empty.

Suddenly I realized once again how there were rules here, that when fishing in certain areas, the fish that is caught must be measured and returned to the waters, depending on the size. In paradise, no such law was adhered to. You catch a snapper, no matter the size, you cleaned it, and you escovitched the same. If the day turned out well, you could even sell a few extras for much needed cash. No tax was levied, and no one forced you in paradise to put your fish back into the sea. I shook my head and continued my walk.

The seagulls, with their wings spread widely and their feet pointed outstretched and fixing to land on water, were aiming for anything that came close to the surface. A little girl was building a sand castle close to the water,

near to a human-made beach area, and each time someone's feet came close to it and threatened to knock down
the foundation, she used her pink shovel and bucket to
steer them away and fiercely protected her handiwork.
Despite her choice of vulnerable location on which to
build, I gave her credit due to her seemingly young age,
her innocence, and the abundance of time she had to
learn and do over. Her determination to build what she
had started and to protect it at all costs, despite everyone
almost stepping on her, was what resonated with me.

Having learned so much from my brief outing, I
dashed toward my car, jumped inside, slid my sunroof
back, and muttered softly: "Be careful where you choose
to lay your foundation, be mindful of people stepping
all over you, and be prepared at all costs to improve on
whatever you've started."

Still puzzled by the meaning inherent in life choices
and the similarity of mottos, I immediately recalled a
story I once heard of a couple who lived on a farm somewhere in the Midwest. Honesty prevailing, I have not
been able so far to acquire any significant personal experience of this region of the country, except to admire the
abundance of rich crops and red meat, which eighteen-
wheelers truck across the country to stock supermarket
shelves.

Anyway, this couple, it has been told, became tired of
tilling the soil on their farm and decided to sell it, using
the money to travel around the world in search of gold.
Now I can't say if the gold was a figurative way of saying

they were looking for riches, or if they were in fact hoping to find the actual chemical element.

After years of searching, the couple became frustrated and had depleted all the funds they had. No riches and no chemical element were found along their travels. One of them, I suspect it was the wife, because that gender is usually more realistic in nature, at least when riches are involved, told the other, that it would make sense to return to the Midwest. The husband agreed; of course, he had no choice because a broke wife would have meant an unhappy life. They arrived, hoping to regain ownership of their old farm with the few funds they had left. As soon as they pulled up to their old farm, they noticed pieces of equipment and people working all over the farmland. Their modest house was torn down, and there was no livestock around. They rushed to speak with the foreman on-site. He explained to them that the farm was not for sale, as the government had gained ownership of it through eminent domain because of the abundance of gold found underground all over the farmland.

The teller of the story did not describe the reaction of the couple, though I remain curious to have known. Well, when I compared the meaning of our mottos, I felt just like this couple should have felt. I went all around the globe from paradise and ended up with the same motto. It did not take long for me to seriously acknowledge that despite the similarities in mottos, it was the disparity in the treatment of subsets that seriously handicapped our abilities to see everyone as being one people.

On my first voyage back to dreamland from paradise after becoming a citizen, I was told "welcome home" by the ICE men.

The term "home" signified a state of belonging; I did not recall any such welcome as an alien resident. All I can recall after handing over that alien passbook were questions about my purpose of travel, who packed my bags, had I visited any plantations or farms, and if so, what vegetable matter was cultivated on said farms. This time, I sped through the customs checkpoint, looking back at the baby strollers being turned upside down, allowing milk bottles to splatter to the floor. All those little brats of alien descent and the elderly alike were not spared from thorough searches for any vegetable matter that they were suspected of possessing inside their belongings. Those little brats were thought by customs to be calculating and very much aware of their rights as automatic citizens since they first appeared on this soil. They had different bills of rights than their parents and were dubbed "anchor babies," a term that implies something hitching something to something else. Just saying. I will not take any credit or rebuke for devising such a term; something about it seems a bit pejorative.

Anyway, the canines stationed at JFK were immediately directed to the line of aliens to sniff out any traces of substances cultivated on the island. It seems they were trained to spot the landing of the orange and cream lovebird more than they were to detect the arrival of any other aircraft. Oh, and the Mexicana and Columbian aircraft as well.

Those cannabis- and coke-sniffing dogs dragged their holders with outstretched arms running behind them through the terminals toward the aliens in the lines, who were already intimidated for being here on earth. The linings of bags were pried up to reveal the white foam padding underneath the nylon after they were thrown onto the table, causing the Appleton White Rum bottles to break.

Medicinal bushes and herbs like Ceresee, brought back to fend off flu symptoms in the cold and the bellyaches and pains, were highly scrutinized and questioned. Then they were confiscated, supposedly to prevent alien insects from being brought in to attack the lovely citrus farms we have here. These farms were ironically being sprayed with potentially harmful pesticides dropped from little planes darting in the skies over the unsuspecting public. Ripe, juicy mangoes were taken away too. Those exiting the airport mumbled in vexation that confiscated insect-infested mangoes were not destroyed in the interest of the public, but rather put on ice (pun intended) for later consumable testing, which would disprove the notion that they were infested in the first place. This suspicion has never been proven, as evidence of insects in the peel or pit has never been found.

Now it was time for me to get over the nostalgia and the flying back and forth, and really buckle down to two or three jobs until such time that the long process for the civil service job came through. That's the other stark difference between here and paradise. Nothing stops for too long. While I'm waiting on one thing, I'm also doing school and about four other things. In paradise, it's mostly one thing at a time; the system is not designed to stress you out.

I'll now describe the place in which I later worked in law enforcement because it bodes heavily on the understanding I later gained about the failing justice system.

The area in question sits just north of the boogie-down Bronx, abutting Yonkers, the city of hills where nothing is on the level, to the west, and New Rochelle lying on Long Island Sound to the north. A couple of villages and towns sit affluently on the outskirts, with their geographical noses turned up. They are usually quiet neighbors, unless there is commercial development next door that increases the flow of traffic through their peaceful streets. Then there would be litigations pending for air pollution, noise pollution, and just general pollution of the peace and sanctity they are so accustomed to enjoying.

So this city in which I served boasted a population density upward of seventy thousand residents sharing a four-square-mile radius. I familiarized myself with its unique geographical, economic, and political characteristics and pondered on the historical origination of its nickname as money-earning Mount Vernon.

There were residual signs of richness, hope, and tranquility of times gone by. But somewhere amid the political changing of the guards, the movement of many young educated folks and talented movie stars leaving, and many businesses moving, economic development had stopped in time. There was still hope on the faces of the residents who believed in its potential. The city had a rich history. It was supposed to be included as a part of New York City back in the late 1800s, but the residents at the time did not want this merger. The city became a place for internal migration of black folks from the south, who were seeking a better life, and incidentally whites from neighboring New York City with a suburban dream.

Contrary to how all of the foregoing information could be perceived, it is not the intent of the writer to imply in any way, shape, or form that Mount Vernon has any characteristics of being a countrified place. The first thing noticeable about suburban countrification is the pace at which things flow. And nothing in Mount Vernon moves at a temperate pace. Just to help you understand: there are no bicycle trails; instead, dirt bikes often times perform wheelies, zipping in and out of regular vehicular traffic on the public roadways. Horseback riding is unheard of, as there are no stables around. Apple picking is an impossibility, as there are no apple trees. The information pointing to diversity could also be misleading, and I understand that wholeheartedly, so again allow me. The city in all fairness could be described as a melting pot, but there were hardly any signs of kumbaya among the different cultural groups. Perhaps this was due to the way each cultural group was stratified.

The racial demographics of the city at the time were strategically scattered by way of some unexplained design. To the far north lived the majority of the whites, of mostly Italian and Jewish descent. For the most part they were unaffected by the goings-on in the other sections of the city, except of course when they were reminded by way of the evening news. They oftentimes referred to the north side by a different name, but trust me, Fleetwood, as serene as it sounds, does fall within the geographical periphery of Mount Vernon.

The south side (which I hold dear, since it was there that I found the Lord), was marked by the division of the Metro North railroad tracks. There lived the majority of the blacks, who were reminded constantly of the historical truths of the nation simply by looking up at the many dedicated street signs in their neighborhoods. These green reflective rectangular signs boasted the names of prominent figures, such as Madison, Monroe, Fulton, Franklin, Jackson, Washington, Harrison, and Martin Luther King. It was on these streets ironically that I was so often reminded of the sacrifices made to rise above crippling social ills and injustices. But you wouldn't think that sacrifices were made in blood and tears on these streets, since an ungrateful few chose to desecrate them by turning them into shooting ranges and drug markets.

On many occasions I drove down these streets with reverence and a feeling of being watched by someone with high expectations. But there were times (almost every Friday and Saturday night) that I quickly ducked my head, not only in shame for the senseless desecration of the place, but also to prevent personal injury from projectiles.

One thing that confused me most was the city government's role in allowing certain conditions on this side of the city to go unchecked, while these same types of practices were never seen on the other sides. A case in point was the existence of residences being sectioned danger-ously into many different pieces by landlords to rent out for profit. It was not uncommon for a single family house to have the closets and boiler room rented to a family of four. These types of conditions were the breeding grounds for some of the emergencies that caused me to run tire-lessly from one 911 call to another. Fighting breaking out when twenty people were lined up in a hallway waiting on a bathroom, or when people were borrowing other people television and scratching the serial numbers off, before moving it to the boiler room down the hallway. I often wondered if the building department inspectors just did not care. I know it was easy for them to see this problem, because it was obvious that a single family house should not have had upward of ten gigantic garbage cans on the sidewalk for the department of public works on any des-ignated garbage collection day. The sheer number of the cans made it obvious that too many families were in there.

There were other signs of neglect demonstrated on this side of the city also. When driving from one call to another, I would notice a few discrepancies with how the taxpayers' money was spent in different parts of the city. For instance, I observed the way the fire hydrants on the south side were covered waist-high with shrubs, which delayed access to the attachment of hoses to put out fires. The firefighters had to perform landscaping duties before they could actually begin to save burning structures. As a result of their bur-dened manpower, they had to continuously call in extra help from nearby jurisdictions to assist. I would be told by the fire department that the fire was deemed suspicious even when no explanations existed to support a theory of foul play. I imagine it was to appease the victims that something was being done, after the fact, and that the justice system was actively working on their cases. For the most part, this resulted in me investigating shrubbery.

On the north side, on the other hand, the areas around the fire hydrants were clean as a whistle and were maintained as such. During periods of snow, the situation was even worse. South-side responses required deicing and weeding, while the snow was cleaned from hydrants on the north side way before any emergencies occurred. Things were done proactively on one side of the city, while on the other side, things were done reactively. During the winter months, streets on the south side melted on their own after a few days following the storm. Streets located on the north end were plowed and salted immediately following the event.

But luckily for the south side, a few institutions of hope and dreams still lived there: the Boys' and Girls' Club (thanks to generous celebrities and others who have made sizable contributions to keep it alive), the Dole Recreation Center (which among other things provides a vibrant meeting place for seniors), the Armory belonging to the forty-second infantry (desperately needing repair to show some appreciation to them), the national historic site of Saint Paul's Church (which has stood with charm since the 1700s, built by the town of Eastchester and later renovated by the same company of geniuses who developed Colonial Williamsburg in Virginia). From the short list of what remains, it should not be difficult to paint a visual picture of our forefathers wrestling in their sleep amid people behaving inappropriately with O.K. Corral auditions on most Fridays and Saturdays.

The west end was home to immigrants from Central America. At the very center were mainly residents from South America and Portugal. They took to the streets seasonally, with pride, bearing their flag-draped cars and honking horns, to celebrate the wins associated with their soccer teams in their native homelands. Morning after morning, the men would congregate at the intersections in the city's center, waiting with their lunch bags and wearing paint-soiled clothes, to be picked up by contractors and landscapers looking for day laborers. They patronized the many businesses owned by their fellow immigrants while they waited to be selected for jobs in their various fields of expertise. On occasions when they weren't picked up at the street corners by contractors, some would spend the day frustrated, drinking Cerveza and sun tanning on the sidewalk. This seemed perfectly normal behavior for them (at least from an immigrant's point of view, where things like these are nonissues abroad). They would get a little bit annoyed when cited for loitering and obstruction of pedestrian traffic on the sidewalk.

The east end was the epicenter of diversity. It consisted of multiple diaspora communities. Every cultural group was represented on the east side. It was fairly uneventful in this area, as the various cultural elements did not seem to have the cohesion to do good or bad for that matter. They simply kept it peaceful and went along with the flow. The few who lived on that side of town who were determined to do wrong trekked across (yes, you guessed it) the tracks to the south side to do same.

Nine-one-one activities, to which my response was required, were designed in accordance with the demographic and geographic compass previously discussed.

Hence, emergency calls that I responded on from the west and center were usually alcohol-infused, with a twist of a sharp object. There is certainly no intention to stereotype here, but it has been my observation that not all immigrants are prone to the same weapon of choice with which to mitigate their differences. Some like sharp objects, and some prefer a more conclusive approach to ending a situation quickly and painlessly.

Disturbances originating in the north to which I responded were usually misunderstandings that occurred at the bars, resulting in a bottle-induced skull fracture at worst or perhaps a bloody lip. After the fight they would usually confess and apologize, then request not to pursue any legal recourse against one another. They couldn't hold their liquor, and they were terrified of going to jail.

The south required my immediate response with the notification of a priest, or in his absence a prayer to a much higher power, due to projectiles from shelling having struck an intended target or an innocent passerby. A call from the south meant follow-up at the trauma center. Jacobi Hospital, which was trusted to work miracles, was the nearest one, and it remained busy. The hospital had a special room for us, in which I spent too many nights waiting for word from the operating room doctor.

In all cases, the ambulances worked a busy schedule. The law-abiding working folks on all sides were either sleeping or too afraid to provide accounts of exactly what had led up to these emergencies.

The eateries apparently were also strategically located in accordance with the same type of seismic shift that resulted in the settling of the racial demographics. I do not believe by any stretch of my imagination that this was purely coincidental. The permits on the north side gave way to banks, insurance companies, and restaurants that served appetizers, main courses, and desserts.

In the center south could be found Popeye's, Mickey Dees, Chicken Hut, Dunkin' Donuts, Papa John's, Dominos, Little Caesar's, Kentucky Fried Chicken, Kennedy, and Mickey Dees again, this time the drive-through for faster fast food.

After dining, for your coronary contentment, you would be able to locate a not-for-profit place of worship in close proximity, usually in the center of the block. A speakeasy was easy to find (no pun intended) in the event you were all churched out and needed a forty-ounce or something stronger to burn the trans fats.

There were some corner stores that sold "loosies" and shot glasses of cocktails to go, in case the consumer was in a hurry. I would be involved in citing these places for their various lawbreaking activities, and they would be permitted by the city to reopen once they re-upped their stock of whatever else they were selling.

All these types of situations perhaps sent a message to some people that some areas were not cared about and, therefore, they were free to add to the existing disorders. I couldn't catch a break in my efforts to get things in order during the midnight shifts when I worked.

It would begin something like this: A dispatcher sounding out of breath on the radio, like someone was chasing her down the middle of the street. I loved the dispatchers, as they usually knew first when trouble was afoot, I could sense destruction and mayhem in their voices. But I knew she was sitting safely behind a console of telephones and computers and all kinds of little red lights and green lights flashing, and her air conditioner was pumping through the ceiling. She was cool and comfortable and out of danger. I continued typing my other seven stabbings and shootings that I caught the night before. She told about half the police officers working in the city to respond on multiple 911 calls of something happening in the Jamaican dialect inside a nightclub on South (yes) Fourth Avenue. She told them she could not decipher what it was because of a language barrier. That just meant more than one Jamaican was speaking at once and in a loud manner in the dialect on the 911 telephone, plus they were drinking and smoking. On the island when speech is compromised by liquor and anything else we would say they are speaking in cursive or join-up. It was impossible for her to understand what they were saying, hence she described it as a language barrier. She kept asking for the first officer who got there to tell her what it was, because she might need to make other notifications. I knew exactly what that meant. Notification to a detective (me). The report I was trying to complete was about a bloody melee that occurred at the same location the night prior.

The victims from that were still in the hospital, and I needed to go speak with them now that they were out of surgery. Most of them would not tell me anything, because they do not "inform" on one another. See, people from paradise say "informer," while Americans say "snitch." Same rule, same motto, just different countries.

I had written violations for their liquor license last night, so I didn't know what they were drinking inside that club tonight. The fire department had taken their certificate of occupancy the night before, so four hundred people should not have been in that club. The building department was notified also that the one route of escape was nailed shut, in violation of all kinds of codes. Yet the club was open for business again in less than twenty-four hours.

The first officer got there, and then the others. I'm guessing they encountered chaos in the streets, with patrons bloodied and some being carried away by their friends, who were not doctors, plus the original problem of the language barrier still existed. The lieutenant on the scene told her over the radio that the club door was locked, and he smelled bleach, and that the officers were trying to stop the vehicles carrying the victims so that the ambulance could take care of them. The cops were telling her that the vehicles would not stop. No one knew what was going on. The lieutenant told her to make the notification (to me). On my way there,

I was thinking, those vehicles would not stop because it was a cultural thing; in paradise we do not wait on ambulances, as there are none coming. The cops chasing these cars did not understand the culture. There was a total disconnect between cultural groups and practices. Serious accidents might occur and further escalate this situation. We could meet them at the hospital in a safe and timely manner. Plus, they might have been driving in a reckless manner to put away anything they had on their persons, which made them more desperate and irrational to drive at whatever speed was required. Chasing them could put the public in further danger. Besides, there would still be a language barrier once they stopped. That's where the misunderstanding was definitely going to occur. If we can't understand what each other is saying, how will the communication take place after the stop? Situations such as these are recipes for disaster. We needed to exercise situational awareness. Pay attention to the social context at which the situation is occurring so that we can respond appropriately. I inform them over the radio to just write the license plates down and forward it to me later or tomorrow after the victims are treated. They are astonished at how calm I am over the situation. I am not excited by this kind of chase.

I arrived, and the lieutenant told me about the bleach. He was also visibly suffering from an adrenaline rush over the tampering with evidence. Yet another person that I needed to calm down. I explained to him that it smelled like Dettol—a powerful disinfectant used on the island to erase all traces of a crime scene. But the door was locked. Someone was possibly inside erasing the video. The owner appeared from down the street, reeking of Dettol and said he hadn't opened the club tonight. All these people running around on the street were having their own party on the sidewalk. No one was informing. The dispatcher said the 911 calls did not come from the telephone inside the club; they came from numbers marked unknown.

The owner opened the door, I went inside, and the place was squeaky-clean. No evidence of a crime scene. The video system was out for repairs, so said the owner. He gave me all his documents from the city, and they were updated since the incident the night before. His certificate of occupancy was pasted on the wall again. The victims being treated each told the same story. They did not hear anything, they did not see anything, and they each felt something warm and a burning sensation. The only part of their story that was different was where they felt the burning sensation.

The building department blamed the fire department. The fire department blamed the state liquor authority. The community blamed the police. The lieutenant wanted to know what the detective was doing to solve these cases… and around and around we went.

I had too many disorders with which to deal, as a result of failing systems. But the state of the criminal justice system was and still is in dire straits. Over the course of my career, I garnered my own perspective regarding the causes of the problems facing the justice system, then and now. Those I'll address later, without jocularity due to their seriousness. Now I must tell you about a couple other jobs I had along this Jamigrant's journey.

Four

Here goes my story about one of the jobs I did along my journey (despite being totally unqualified). The lack of qualification was not my fault, as the vetting process was not thoroughly done. It was a situation where I was not asked if I could do X-Y-Z, so I did not tell. It was perfectly legal at the time, even within our armed forces, which has since changed that primitive practice.

I joined the large group of immigrants who became caregivers to the homebound and who provided companionship for the elderly. This was perhaps one of the quickest certifications one could get, but I chose to forgo the required certification and delve right into a self-imposed on-the-job-training. The plan was not to take this along a professional pathway, as I was well aware that being a full-fledged nurse required a special calling. The medical field had not specifically called me.

So on one of those mornings when we all wake up to the pace of nothing moving and everything taking too damn long, I began to rummage through the classified section of the newspaper. I came across an ad that called for a companion to a homebound woman. The ad listed just one requirement with which I was not familiar: skill in operating a Hoyer Lift. There was no Internet at my disposal at the time to look it up, and I just figured it would be something I could quickly learn how to operate. I ignored the requirement and answered the ad. Jamigrants are used to ignoring things that seem like minor details to them; hence saying, "no problem, man," to everything, whether trivial, complex, or not understood.

The telephone was answered politely by a lady who identified herself as the person whom I would be relieving at eight o'clock each morning. She would be returning at eight o'clock each evening to relieve me. This is another thing about paradise: if you are waiting on any job to be relieved (don't wait), it is likely that the relief will not show up. Why go somewhere to do something if somebody else is already there doing it? Just doesn't make sense on the island. She quickly went down a list of what was required of me during the day, and without reservation I acknowledged that the maneuvering of the Hoyer Lift for bath time and wheelchair transfer for a quick stroll would be no problem whatsoever. After she explained to me that the day-girl had suddenly quit and that the patient could not be left alone, I immediately jumped to the occasion to begin working the following morning at eight o'clock sharp. She advised me to wear white, I guess to pretend that I was acting in a professional capacity. So I donned my tight white jeans and a white linen shirt (the only thing I had in pure white), which I had worn to an all-white reggae boat ride a few Saturdays prior.

I arrived fifteen minutes early and was met at the door by the same woman with whom I had spoken on the telephone. After exchanging warm smiles and pleasantries, she escorted me to meet the patient, who was still in bed and was not particularly in a talkative mood. This was understandable as it was still early, and from the introduction, she had a set morning routine, which involved a bath, then coffee, a little break, then breakfast, and perhaps a stroll in her wheelchair, weather permitting. The only thing that was not made clear, though I later found out the hard way, was that "weather permitting" meant she loved to be out during heavy snow. The woman was an avid skier until she became bedridden by a debilitating illness. But let's just back up a minute. In paradise, whenever someone says, "weather permitting," it means, "if there is no rain." Simple. There is no snow, hail, nor tornadic activity in paradise, so a thunderstorm is the only precipitation that can be expected there. No one wishes away the sunshine there. But with all the choices here, of what could likely fall out of the sky, we become so presumptuous that we hope there will be no sunshine. It appears that the more choices we are given, the more demanding we become. I'll tell you later about the day

I found out that the sun was not her first love, but for now, I need to finish the introductory process. I quickly shifted my attention to the layout of the place, as I did not want to make her uncomfortable by insisting she engage in conversation with a stranger who had invaded her bedroom so early in the morning.

My eyes darted to the far corner of the room, opposite the bed. There was a set of six circular steps leading toward a claw-foot tub, which was nestled in a sunken Ensuite. Overlooking the tub was a double-hung, paned with half-moon, colored-glass window. I inadvertently lifted my finger to point at a contraption that was positioned in the general area of the tub, not because I intended to show it to anyone, but because it appeared strange and looked more or less like a hammock that seemed out of place. Without realizing that I was actually pointing at the machine, the woman conducting the introduction stated, "Oh yes, the Hoyer Lift, it's generally kept over there when it's not in use." My finger, which was still extended, slowly retracted into place, and my hand dropped to my side, limp. I immediately thanked the dear Lord that I had not shown my ignorance by referring to the lift as a hammock and asked Him quickly if it were His will that I should admit the untruth I had told about knowing how to operate this piece of equipment. For some reason still unknown, that prayer went unanswered, and I continued to pay attention to my orientation.

My level of distraction and fear was mounting. There was just nothing self-explanatory about the operation of this thing in the room, and the truth was that I had never even seen a picture of something like it before. We did not have them in paradise. The closest thing to a Hoyer Lift in paradise at the time was four men holding the four corners of a sheet on the short sides of the fabric, gently swaying it to the desired location and gently resting the elderly down. For all the years I had witnessed this done, no elderly person had ever sustained an injury. There was no space consumed in the bedroom by any bulky equipment, as the sheet was neatly folded and put away right after use. It was like a quick lullaby for the bedridden, but one that seemed much more personable than a hammock-like machine with a crank attached to it. I needed a training course in the safe operation of this thing, and fifteen minutes was more than enough time to talk about the collective duties I had to perform.

After all, how much can you tell me about emergency contact numbers on the refrigerator door, or cereal, fruits, vegetables, and pasta? The medication was already organized in little boxes marked Sunday, Monday, Tuesday, Wednesday, and so on. There was no thinking involved in administering the tablets, except a knowledge of the day of the week. The instruction was to give the pills with juice or water at lunchtime. I had heard enough of what to prepare and where to find it. Darn, common sense dictated that I look in the kitchen, either in the refrigerator or the cupboard, for any form of food kind.

I politely told the woman I understood where to find the numbers and food supply, and directed her attention back to the unfamiliar Hoyer Lift. To my horror, she quickly dismissed my concern by letting me know that the patient was not yet ready to get out of bed; otherwise she would have quickly shown me the preferred way of transferring her from the bed. However, whatever way I opted to do it would be fine. Opted? I knew that meant to make a choice from a range of possibilities. I saw no possibility of even attempting to hoist any human being from the comfort and safety of her bed by way of this thing, let alone devising different options or choices by which to commit such an unthinkable act. Fifteen minutes flew by so quickly, and it was now eight o'clock. Time for us to wrap up the introduction, bid our good-byes, and part ways until eight in the evening.

I nervously locked the door and returned to the bedroom, dreading the moment when it was bath time. Trying desperately not to say or do anything that would suggest an eagerness for the patient to get out of bed, I began to say how cozy it was to have the opportunity to sleep in and relax while the sunlight reflected many shapes and hues through the colored-glass window. My conversation was one-sided except when she asked me to turn the radio on. The station was already preset to 10/10 WINS, and she listened attentively to the brief excerpts of news reports that covered just about every serious event around the city in less than ten minutes. The report quickly changed to the weather, and snow was in the forecast for late afternoon. At the mention of snow, her face illuminated in a smile. I smiled broadly as well, believing with all my heart that this meant a later-than-usual sleep, with perhaps breakfast in bed, a sponge down instead of a transfer to the claw-foot tub, and no stroll outside as the weather was clearly not forecasted to permit. I was finding a way to buy time until evening, when I planned on remaining on my own time after eight so that I could observe my relief use the lift. The night girl was responsible for the second bath time of the day, so if God could just help me to bypass the morning bath and the stroll, I would have been eternally grateful. It was during these times in life, when faced with the toughest of challenges, that we always promise God that we would sin no more (like lying about our skills) if He could only help us this one last time.

Before my smile could dissolve or my ardent prayer could pass beyond the vaulted ceilings in the bedroom, my patient energetically shouted, "Up, up, up, get me up," and pointed to the lift. Not wanting to seem as if I was reluctant, I again mentioned how perfect the weather was for a little-longer-than-usual sleep. She ignored me totally and repeated her request with a very eager tone, and a dash of impertinence by addressing me as a dwarf. Remembering Mammie once again, I ignored her salutation and decided to stand tall. I walked over to the lift and wheeled it over toward the bed and up a side ramp located next to the steps. Up until that point I was clearly uncertain (short of a miracle) how to get the patient from the bed onto this thing. I was terrified as to what my next move should be. I bought some time, about two minutes of it, fumbling with the pillows, then the sheet, and then moving a food tray from the nightstand. Suddenly my blood pressure dropped a notch (just enough to prevent the impending stroke) when I heard the intercom from the doorman.

It appeared he hated being referred to as a doorman and much preferred the title of concierge, which was consistent with similar persons on the affluent east side of Manhattan. He introduced himself thus when I first met him in the lobby and repeated it, with much emphasis on the word "concierge." Regardless of his duties, functions, and pay scale, which qualified or disqualified him for the title of doorman or concierge, I thought he still deserved the latter. If only for the fact that he carried himself in a remarkably neat manner, with a crisp khaki suit trimmed with broad red stripes running down the sides of the trousers and around his hat. Clean-shaven and polite, he appeared to be generously tipped to open taxi doors for the residents. He looked important.

So, the concierge rang, and I was thrilled to answer. I hoped that maybe a package had been delivered and I could buy some more well-needed time opening it, retrieving the contents for her, and discussing with interest and in detail whatever the contents were. But someone watching over me had a greater plan. This has been my case along my life's journey so far. Every time I prayed for something and gave God a plan with the prayer, He would respond with a better plan for me—one that I hadn't even known existed. So now, I have grown to realize and trust Him by telling Him what matter of a pickle I have gotten myself in and that I have no plan of how I would solve the problem. It's all up to Him. I have never ever been disappointed.

As I answered the intercom, the concierge said, "I am escorting the visiting nurse upstairs." I glanced quickly at the refrigerator and saw the magnet holding down the paper with the visiting nurse's schedule. Yup, she was due today. Who better to know how to maneuver a Hoyer Lift? I was going to insist that bath time not be interrupted and finagle a way to get the nurse to assist me with the lift. I thanked the concierge for delivering this angel to me and welcomed her with the firmest handshake and smile I ever had. I quickly informed her (lest she believed she was leaving anytime soon) that the bath that I had run was getting cold and that I was in the process of getting my patient in the tub.

The nurse was quite cooperative, and I walked over to test the water's temperature. Acting amazed at how rapidly the water was cooling, I asked her if she minded just placing my patient in the lift while I got the towels. She did not mind at all. I paid close attention to every move and maneuver and the cranking of the lift until it arrived at its destination in no time at all. It was the smoothest operation of any machinery that I had witnessed. This was indeed an intensive training course that I had just received, and every bit of what I had just witnessed had to be retained. I quickly administered the bath, applied her lavender body mist and her robe, and shouted to the nurse, "She is all yours." I sounded confident and chirpy, but at the same time I was praying that she would come hitherto. The moment I saw her little white shoes in the corner of my eyes, I immediately began to act busy to bring the bathroom back to its pristine condition. The kindly nurse again obliged, and I took in every detail of the crash course involving the transfer of the patient back to the bed via the lift.

Despite being tremendously relieved that I could now safely perform the job for which I was hired, it was clear that the phrase "no problem" was germane only to paradise. It should not be arbitrarily used by Jamigrants, especially oversees. Seeing everything as potentially not a problem might result in serious bodily harm to someone and land you right in the middle of a litigious situation. This woman, I later learned, had a fierce barrister who kept a close eye on every mishap, especially those pertaining to her care. Had the nurse not arrived or another unforeseen miracle manifested itself, I would have landed in a serious problem. One perhaps that I would have been paying for up until this day, both with time and money (which I did not possess). The rest of the nurse's time was spent on performing her own checkups and follow-ups with the patient, and somehow the patient decided to cancel her outdoor plans and spend the rest of the day indoors, like I had initially hoped. I did not question her reason for canceling, and frankly did not want to breach the subject.

So I escaped the prison sentence and the tort, and my operation of the Hoyer Lift became a piece of cake.

But then came that day when I would pay for all my sins all at once. Remember, I promised that I would tell you about it? The one when I found out the hard way that my patient really loved the snow and that she always wished that the weather would permit it? Yes, that one.

I woke up extra early in order to relieve the night girl, the one who had shared some culpability in landing me in the Hoyer Lift fiasco. I was not operating on island time, which is usually about two hours behind the normal time on the clock. I hurried to the number two train because the weather was permitting upward of a foot of snow, accompanied by high winds. Not quite a blizzard by any standard in the northeast, but for people accustomed to sun all the time, this could tend to be a traumatic event. We tend to go through changes and lack of peaceful sleep during the night because we are accustomed to be excused from work in paradise in the event it rains too hard. Moderate to heavy rain showers on the island generate an unwritten understanding that a person (regardless of the profession) may, or most likely may not, show up to work. Just to illustrate how that works. If you should have business such as a surgery scheduled at the nearest hospital and it is raining heavily, you would most definitely show up in order to get the problem taken care of to prolong your life. However, when you arrived to be admitted, the receptionist would explain in a casual but friendly manner that, "Dr. Wilson did not come in today, I guess because of the rain. You have to come back next Wednesday for the heart surgery." If you did not plan on being around next Wednesday due to the ailing heart, she would gladly cancel your appointment (no problem whatsoever) and would tell Dr. Wilson not to worry about the surgery. So now you understand that if possible cardiac arrest is treated in such a trivial manner, it shouldn't be alarming that places such as police stations, the post office, gas stations, and so forth could potentially face rain-related closures in paradise.

But putting aside my island upbringing with the perks to which I had grown accustomed, I showed up on time for my relief because my patient could not be left alone. Things seemed a tad bit unusual when I entered, as her outfit for the day was draped over her wheelchair, which was positioned conspicuously almost in the center of the bedroom. Her breakfast tray had crumbs from toast and a half-filled glass of orange juice on it. Strange. All these occurrences had taken place before my arrival. Unsure of what had triggered this early rising and preparation, I looked curiously to the night girl, who was putting her coat on to leave. She advised me that my patient preferred to go out early so as not to miss the excitement of being in the eye of the impending snowstorm. Lord, have mercy! Here I was, rushing to arrive indoors before the first flake fell out of the sky, only to be told that I would spend the day outdoors in the center of it all. Her excitement to get out into this mini blizzard was the same excitement I was so accustomed to feeling when going to the beach in paradise on an obviously warm and sunny day.

We completed the morning ritual, and the elevator operator pressed "L" on the console for us, allowing us to descend into the lobby. The concierge held the door, and we rolled out of the foyer of the building and headed southbound on Park Avenue. Just an aside: elevators are not popular concepts for residential facilities on the island, but in places where we do utilize them, we are usually able to press our own buttons. I was thinking that an elevator button pusher would not show up to work in paradise when it rained, or the sun shone for that matter, after they accepted that prestigious job. They would just show up on payday to collect the check with no problem at all. Who in paradise would seriously call to complain that they were inconvenienced by pushing a button? And who would they call?

Anyway, we proceeded along our way and concentrated our travel west on Madison, then over to Lexington, and so on and so forth, with brief stops at unique shops along the way. We stopped at her favorite ice cream (yes, cold dessert) shop and bakery, and she requested a sundae with all the trimmings. I showed her all the contents of the bags containing the expensive little trinkets we had gathered along the way thus far, and by then we had lost touch with time.

The wind had picked up speed from the south, and the snow had started to deliver its promise. After repacking all the stuff carefully and individually rewrapping them in tissue paper, she paid for the dessert, bottles of water, and whatever other gourmet pastry that had caused the check to be equivalent to half my entire week's pay. It was time to leave the bakery.

Wisdom would have dictated, or so I thought, that if everything around you were covered in white fluffy snow and the wind was hampering your vision, then the most logical decision would be homeward bound. So, of course, upon reaching the exit to the sidewalk canopy, I presumptuously turned right, onto Park Avenue's one-way, against the flow of southbound traffic. My direction of travel was quickly corrected by my patient, who requested that we head downtown. I could feel that the traction was no longer smooth under the wheels of the chair, and I had a strong feeling that another quarter of an inch of this white stuff on the ground would prove disastrous for us. Having this vision of a "Catastrophe on Park" (the newspaper headline), I double-checked if she had made a mistake in changing my initial direction toward home. No. She quite intended to implement the change of direction in order to further enjoy the rest of the day in the storm.

Pedestrians who hustled past us to reach their respective destinations safely indoors began to turn their heads to look at me in wonderment. I could read their thoughts about me being obviously cruel to have allowed, despite the early warnings of the weather people, such an event to catch us outdoors. Their eyes told the story that they were certain of the fact that no one else was culpable for this atrocity than the woman holding the handles and sliding behind the chair. I was too afraid of how this propulsion of the chair was going to end to even waste my other emotions on telling these uninformed stuck-up judges to mind their own damn business.

But then my fright went up one notch in the realm of petrophilia when I received a sudden request to make a left and cross the street. Under normal circumstances, dry pavement permitting, this would have been a non-event. But the wheels of the chair were caked with snow, which had transformed itself to ice. They were operating totally under the control of the element and were rolling like circular popsicles—the chair skating along, with me partially sliding behind it. Any sudden turn, jerk, or maneuver could potentially send both driver and passenger airborne, with the chair landing on both of us. I tried to caution against the idea of making this left turn but was immediately overruled and was forced into making it. Crossing the street was another fear I was yet to deal with, as the visibility of the drivers was clearly impaired. I couldn't even see them, so I knew for sure they couldn't see us either.

Immediately upon turning, the left wheel penetrated the snow and proceeded to dip below what I initially saw as the snow-covered crosswalk. The other wheel was in the air and clearly visible high above the ground. My patient was now leaning out of the chair toward the wheel that I could hardly see. I could not decide if the safety straps were doing any good by holding her waist down in the seat, or whether these straps had become dangerous by not being able to hold her torso in place. The tension against the straps had caused them to be tightly hidden somewhere in her lap, and regardless of my feelings about their safety at that moment, I couldn't have unfastened them even if I wanted to. I began to pull, push, and scream for help. A couple of well-intentioned passersby rushed to our assistance. They began to push and pull as well. The wheel was stuck. One of the men also had the same question as I had about the seat belt, but the other one quickly cautioned him not to unfasten it, as that could have resulted in us not being able to hold my patient in the lopsided chair.

The nearest pay-phone call box was half a block down the street. Cell-phone availability was scarce at the time, and the weather would not have guaranteed any signal to make a call in any case. The call box was our only option, but all three of us were holding various things under temporary control and could not relinquish our grasps. A third Good Samaritan ran to the call box to call 911. Within minutes (which seemed like hours), an ambulance arrived with a police car in tow. They extracted my patient from the wheelchair by cutting the safety straps and lifting her to a gurney onto the ambulance. The police officers loaded the wheelchair with the twisted wheel into the trunk of their car and rode behind the ambulance to the hospital. I, although eager to get the all-clear from the doctor inside the emergency room that my patient was physically unhurt, was also cognizant that as per protocol, her attorney must immediately be notified in the event of any emergencies or unusual occurrences that involved her. I retrieved his telephone number from her purse and asked the nurse's permission to use the hospital telephone. His secretary answered and initially began to lie about a meeting that he was in, but the mention of my patient's name quickly brought said meeting to an end, with him cutting in, "I have it, Connie." Before I could finish the sentence explaining that we were stuck in a hole at the crosswalk and we were transported via ambulance to St Vincent Hos…he told me he was on his way and terminated the call. His anticipated arrival was the longest wait I had ever endured.

The officers began to admonish me on the dangers of taking anyone whose mobility was challenged outdoors when the weather had been predicted to be this bad. I tried to explain to them that from a cultural point of view, I would not even have made the decision to take myself outdoors given such a prediction. This weather had not given me any permission to even come to work. The idea was one that had fallen within the scope of my duties. They still felt the need to explain the meaning of "endangerment and negligence" to me.

Their lecture was interrupted by the arrival of the barrister, who introduced himself and asked whether there was any defect in the sidewalk, crosswalk, or roadway. The officers looked stunned, and I believe for the first time they were on the same page as I was. How is it that he did not question whether his client had sustained any injury? One of the officers sarcastically told him that she was OK and was just being checked out as a precaution. I quickly looked at him in shock. Precaution? This was unheard of in paradise. Whenever something happens, either you are hurt, or you are not hurt. No one transports you anywhere to get checked out as a precaution. Hospitals are busy places for the very seriously ill, and precautions are not handled there. If you did not show any signs of bleeding or a limb was not separated from the rest of your body, then the diagnosis would naturally be, "You very lucky, and careful next time." That would be the end of that. But in the case under discussion, the lawyer quickly snapped back, "My client may be physically OK; but for a likely defect in the roadway, she most certainly would not have fallen out of her chair." The "but for" was a sure indication that a lawsuit was imminent for the psychological part of it. He demanded photographs of the location and would be following up for a detailed police report on the matter. One of the officers interrupted his demands by insinuating that perhaps the idea to put his client in such a vulnerable situation was ill-advised. Now this cop was dragging me into this mess. Whereupon to my delight, the astute attorney snapped back, "She is entitled to enjoy the life she has been accustomed to, and that includes a stroll in the snow; she was an avid skier." He was so on point with that, but more importantly, I was ecstatic that he knew this was her idea and that I did not deliberately put her in harm's way by circumventing the weather forecast. This preview of his opening statement pertaining to this litigation was pointing more toward me being a witness than a defendant. But this still wasn't fair, because there were two victims involved here. I felt like pushing my luck now by request-ing a medical checkup as a precautionary measure. This type of checkup, which I had never dreamed about in paradise, would provide me some needed psychological help regarding the trauma I too had endured. Not want-ing to be grilled on the stand about my qualifications pertinent to this job I had undertaken without proper vetting, I decided to endure the trauma and remain a witness. After all, I was blessed twice, once with respect to the operation of the Hoyer Lift and then with the naviga-tion of the wheelchair. There would not be a third time for me. I moved on to the next gig in the life of a resilient immigrant—a Jamigrant. Incidentally, Kenny Rogers had always been one of my favorite country singers, so I most definitely knew "…when to walk away and when to run." This gig was a gamble; I kicked up my heels and ran.

Five

A Gig

One thing that you may or may not have picked up on is that I, like most immigrants, am a jack-of-all-trades, and to be fair, we are all masters of some. But nothing remains too large or too small for us to do. It is also very difficult for anyone to detect when we are doing something for the first time. We present to be very confident and knowledgeable, to the point wherein we are able to convince you that this is just a better way of doing whatever it is.

Case in point: I took on this gig to oversee the operations of a club and cafe. The owner of the business had his hands full with another similar business, which he also owned, so I was working alongside a few other people to get this particular business going. I had no prior business experience, except of course as a customer. The extent of the duties entailed emptying the cash registers at given times, checking when food needed to be replenished, and scheduling the disc jockey, cook, and bartenders. The liquor was transported from the other store in boxes, so I didn't have to keep inventory on those.

This type of business was new to me, and initially it felt like I was going out to party when I was actually going to work. Music was the center of the operation, and if there is anything to be learned about a Jamigrant, it is that staying still is not an option for us when music is playing. We will rush to the dance floor like someone is chasing us. No partner is necessary.

Whenever I had locked the money away, maybe three or four times per night depending on how much the crowd was drinking, I would respond to the music Jamigrant style. A dress code was never discussed, so again I had the option to dress, yes, you guessed it, in true Jamigrant style. For anyone not quite familiar with that, the best description I can give is any style that incorporates significantly less fabric than the average clothing. We conserve on material in paradise because the thing is expensive, and it does nothing other than conceal pure beauty and generate heat.

The gig was easy; there was nothing to complain about except that the bartenders were unreliable. People would show up ready for their liquor to aid them in unwinding from the various stressors they had run away from, and the bartenders would claim they messed up on the schedule. Bartenders, as we all know, play an integral part in any business. They do much more than concoct the brews. They are therapists. To be fair to them, they are really psychiatrists in their own right. They listen to the afflicted, give advice, and also administer the drug: alcohol by the glass. Needless to say that whenever they were absent, there were just too many afflicted people waiting impatiently for their medication.

Being able to think on my feet, I derived a permanent solution for this problem of constant absenteeism on the part of the bartenders. After discussing that for an added bonus, and in addition to my already specified duties, I would gladly fill the vacant bartender slots as needed, the position was granted to me, with no vetting whatsoever. I had never personally mixed any alcoholic beverages to drink beyond a margarita, and perhaps white rum with a chaser. In fact, the first time I took a real look at the liquor shelves, I was confused as to what drinks Triple Sec, Madori, and some other colorful liquors were supposed to be used for. Plus, I was oblivious as to which drink it was that I needed to set ablaze with a lighter. That fire in the glass always seemed amazing to me, but I was quite aware that alcohol, fire, and an untrained bartender could spell significant trouble. I was clearly not a qualified liquorholic.

Knowing that quick on-the-job-training was needed, I bought myself a little book called the *Bartender's Handbook* and placed it under the counter next to the ice maker. Patients shouldn't see anyone researching their medication before dispensing it. That just didn't seem right, so I intentionally kept the book out of sight. But there is always a little glitch to put a wrench into people's plans whenever they believe they have things down pat. The darn lighting under the counter was not quite bright enough to illuminate the print in the handbook. Besides, the book was resting so low under the counter that it was almost impossible to read. Even the simplest drink was a problem for me to mix without a guide, as the ingredients just were not familiar. Besides, I was a bit confused as to how much of each liquor should be poured out of that spout on the bottles. More disturbing was that the rule of what should be shaken and what should be stirred seemed so ridiculous from the island's point of view. Back in paradise, the drinkers made the simple decision whether they wanted to stir the brew or gulp it down the way it was served. Here, we have to tell someone how to get drunk?

Then there were the picky ones with requests such as ice cubes. crushed ice or no ice at all, and strained. It took me a few weeks to realize that the term "neat," not only meant no ice in the glass, but it also meant no chilling at all. In paradise it's simple; we serve ice in everything, and you take the ice out if it's watering down the liquor. Why do these people here persist on driving both themselves and the untrained bartender crazy by thinking about all these variances? If something is bothering me to the point where I need a drink and also need to lay my troubles out to a perfect stranger behind a bar, then my mind would be on the thing that's bothering me, not the ice in the liquor.

My book was inaccessible for the most part, so winging it was my only option. I mixed whatever the hell I could remember and watched the drinkers' lips purse and eyes squeeze shut whenever they tasted something that was too strong, had too much lemon juice in it, or was just completely opposite to the taste they were expecting. As soon as they regained their consciousness from the first sip, I would convincingly tell them it was the island version of whatever drink they had ordered. Everyone loved the island version and soon started to order it. The book became obsolete, and I became an expert at mixing.

Counseling on various topics—such as divorce, cheating, spying (on significant others), weight gain, loss of a pet, unruly children, wives shopping excessively, back pains from sleeping on the couch (an aftereffect of cheating), and many others—became my other area of expertise. The advice I gave on these issues seemed to be good, because people ordered more island versions and gave me updates on how their issues were being resolved.

There was this one frequent drinker. I remember his name was Vinny, and he was one of those high rollers who tipped big, to the point where I had to check with him to verify if he intended to leave that much money on the counter. I was not complaining about the tip by any means; it was just that the amount was always more than the sum total of the drinks he had consumed. The only problem Vinny needed counseling for was whether or not he should get another blue Corvette or a black one for a change. He always started off his drinking with a shot.

The first night he came in, Vinny requested a pony of De Leon La Leona. I thought he was talking in a foreign language but didn't dare show the ignorance that was hiding behind my smile. The pony and any relation to my present job was clearly something I had never heard of before, so I was dealing with that part of his request in my head before I even addressed the other part. Glasses and bottles were familiar in the context of a speakeasy, while to me, ponies were a little bit strange, as it indicated an animal that Vinny could ride. Being cornered behind a counter with nowhere to run was not a place I necessarily wanted to be at that particular moment. I tried to find the answer in my book.

I bent down under the counter, nervously flipped to the glossary at the back of the book, and under bartenders' jargon, it said a pony was a shot. What a relief to suddenly realize that Vinny was in fact not harboring any ideas about RWD (riding while drunk). This was just unnecessary complication for someone to use this term to a person from the island. By simply using the word "shot," I could have been spared all that pain and undue suffering.

Anyway, I looked on the shelf for the Deleon thing and saw it nestled among the pricier bottles. A quick peek at the price list revealed it was not cheap. I knew right away that Vinny was both complicated and rich. It was that first night also that I noticed he never asked the amount of his check when he was ready to leave for the night, so I attempted to return the excess, which I thought was clearly a mistake of drunkenness. But he was quite sober. He was just complicated, like most people here, who were rich.

It was truly fun while it lasted, but the mixing of brews and music thumping all night in my head was not something I could have dealt with over a long period of time. The clientele began to migrate to less remote locations, where they didn't have to drive too far while drunk. This, for me, was one more set of experiences gained from a gig, which I would only revisit due to some measure of extreme financial brokenness.

As a Jamigrant it was always wise to keep the experiences and know-hows of all the gigs along the way, just in case there was ever a need for a temporary job to stop an immediate gap. At one point I even had a trunk-full of canvass sneakers which I used crazy glue to decorate with glitters, rhinestones and buttons. I was selling these like hot potatoes on my break-time in the lounge of the Telephone Company. The turn-over from my sales was great, but my fingers took a beating from the crazy glue, leaving little dents and holes in my skin. The important thing though, was the repertoire of skills I had amassed by practicing to be, bartender and counselor, shoe designer, home-health aid, telephone service and equipment provider and still my list was growing.

Six

POLICE ACADEMY 98TH SESSION

My initial thought while preparing to report to the Police Academy in January of all months, was that the devil had gotten word that I was still harboring some kind of island-derived mentality towards the winter months. He was determined to rid me once and for all, of this ill-will which I harbored for temperature which fell below eighty degrees Fahrenheit. He even played a trick on me, by whispering that training would probably be more or less limited to the indoor gyms and shooting ranges due to the accumulation of snow, ice and freezing temperatures. This devil was a liar then, now and forever shall be.

I entered the Academy classroom with my fellow Recruits, and from the sound of silence, I knew that we all felt too new to speak. We were already forewarned prior to our Swearing-In Ceremony that things would be all uphill from that point onwards, and we had endured speeches of what was to be expected during training and the probationary period. Much of the talk and planning were centered around equipment, uniform, physical training gear, lectures involving the law, and examinations which we were expected to pass. Emphasis was placed on qualification exercises involving firearms, emergency vehicle operation, CPR, and various simulation exercises involving the application of appropriate tactics in response to emergency situations. I was comfortable with the fact that these were going to be intensive and rigorous, and I had mentally prepared myself to endure them.

Most of us if not all had received varying degrees of pep talk from other police officers who were family members or friends. All of us had passed the Physical Agility Test. I was in good shape and had been exercising for months in preparation for training. I felt confident that I was more than ready for physical training.

So we were there in the classroom and the Orientation process was about to get underway. There was the sound of someone whistling and advancing from the rear of the room, but our necks and stares remained fixed to the podium in front of us. No one was flinching. He occupied the podium and surveyed the room quietly. Then with an inaudible sound of "Attention" with every syllable dragged out, he commanded us to our feet. He then mumbled, "At ease, sit" and we sat. He gave his name, which sounded at first like "Heckler," which would have been quite fitting, but in actuality his name had no "L" in it. His first question was, "Who is present from Mount Vernon?" Those who identified with that specified group, which included me, held our arms up. His response was a deep groan of 'UUHM," which carried with it a feeling that it translated into, "you have no idea what you're in for." It was clear that the city had a reputation that 'guts' was needed to protect and serve therein. Everyone in law enforcement circles knew that Recruits being trained for service in Mt Vernon, were entitled to a little extra divine intervention than Recruits from other jurisdictions. We realized much later on that this particular set which we were now a part of, did not discuss things as trivial as pick-pocketing and so forth when they did field training. They returned from field training discussing kidnappings and other manners of evil. The deep groan was Hecker's way of expressing compassion for us and we appreciated it.

His face had that look like he was the bearer of bad news, in a mischievous way. His main duty was to explain all the rules, and to ensure we were in full compliance even when he had forgotten to explain the existence of a particular rule. The first set of instructions were directed at anyone who hadn't received the memo before show-ing up that morning. Return to the locker room and remove all earrings and other types of jewelry. Maintain only a wrist watch which was black in color including the band. Remove all traces of make-up including colored lip gloss. Remove all braids and hair ornaments. Pull hair back and contain it in a bun if it was below the nape of the neck. Remove all fake nails and nail polish. Remove all non-prescription glasses or contact lenses. Return in exactly fifteen minutes.

He proceeded to go over a litany of rules and regulations which included what to do as a Recruit, even when you were in your bed and heard a suspicious sound in your dreams. All actions, thoughts, feelings and expressions were now governed by the new status of being a police officer in training. Of utmost importance was that, the misstep of one Recruit would result in the entire group being reprimanded. It was also important to remember at all times that any action taken by the Recruit with the best of intentions, and said action just happened to turn out badly, that you would be terminated. In other words, if you tried to save someone from drowning then that person should not drown regardless of the strength of the current. Cleaning assignments and frequent inspections of locker rooms, garbage cans, kitchenettes, bathrooms, floor tiles, gym, uniforms, and the parking lot were to be expected. All these things were fairly reasonable disciplines which I had no doubt that I could have accomplished. We got through orientation, memorized the rules and regulations, policies and procedures and signed for our manual which contained the same things, but in written form. A few guest speakers occupied the rest of the day, and although the interior of the building was freezing cold, it was better than being outdoors in January. The guest speakers were from varying police departments, but each one upon entering, requested to know who the recruits from Mt Vernon were.

On the second day and the days which were to follow, physical training went into full gear. I realized then, that I was not the only one, who believed that the near zero temperature was going to be a factor of consideration while in the Academy. The bearer of bad news, this time wearing a smirk on his face, instructed us to change into our physical-training attire and report to an area just outside the gym. Everyone, turned up wearing the assigned grey sweat pants and shirt with our names in bold on the back, with all kinds of thermal underwear peeping out from underneath, and of course a jacket since the meeting area was outdoors. Without any delay or further confusion, we were immediately sent back to the locker rooms to remove every garment except the sweatshirt and matching pants. While in the locker room, there were mumbles being exchanged about matters concerning hyperthermia and inhumane treatment. However, once we got back outside all of those discussions were over and appeared as if they had never occurred. We stood in line listening to instructions about running in cadence, and instructions about the route we were going to take while remaining in formation. Directing this operation was a retired United States Marine, who seemed as if he was oblivious to the fact that everyone standing in line was already frozen like a statue.

My toes grew numb. I had no feeling in my fingers, but I was still slightly coherent enough to understand that the distance which we were going to run, according to the instructions, was of grave concern for me in that type of weather. According to the instructions of the Marine, we were going to take a three and a half mile run, which would begin up an incline and away from the Academy grounds. Then return (not via ambulance) but by running an additional three and half miles. While running we were supposed to be singing these running cadence songs which would be taught to us by the Marine as we went along our route. The cadence songs, among other reasons, were supposed to keep us in formation or "dressed," and moving to the same beat or rhythm, which at normal speed was a quick-time march, and at running speed, a double-time march. I was concerned about being able to do quick or double without some form of medical emergency setting in. A seven-mile run even under moderate weather conditions was at best, very challenging for me.

We started off in a trot and were repeating the words of the cadence song as we approached the incline less than a quarter of a mile from where we had started. I felt as if I could have run over the incline if I was running and carrying just my weight. However, it felt as if an elephant was seated comfortably on my chest with its hind legs crossed. I began to slowly drop out of formation. The instructor began to run alongside me shouting the words of the cadence song more loudly in my ears, as an indication for me to pick up the pace. Everything in me wanted to, but this is where as Jamaicans would say, "mi heart willing but mi body was weak." At some point nearing the end of the first two miles, I started walking with the entire group ahead of me, some running, some still moving at least at a trot, and some doing a combination of running and walking. Another instructor joined with me to 'motivate' my movement. Each time as the elephant shifted position, I was able to double-time, then came right back to the snail's pace. My mind was now fixed on just surviving an eminent cardiac arrest than it was on accomplishing anything else that I had dreamed for in life.

I continued along the route, not only carrying my elephant, but also a monkey that was now on my shoulders whispering something about being female and failing from the group that needed to have guts. At some point I saw the rest of my fragmented group, no longer in cadence, passing me on the opposite direction going back towards the Academy. I had not yet reached the three-and-a-half-mile point where I was supposed to have made the loop back. The instructor was still by my side making sure that I arrived there, as long as I had a pulse.

Through some miracle and occasional collapsing on the side of the road, I arrived back, in a matter of what seemed like hours to find my group doing push-ups to compensate for my failure in completing the run in a timely fashion. I was instructed to join in the push-ups, since I was still showing signs of being alive, and immediately thereafter, get dressed into regular uniform and report for a conference with the commanding officer of the Academy. Conference was swift and to the point. My entire future was discussed in less than five minutes. The pressure was on. I was determined more than ever to run, but I had no control over this weather which was only going to get more frigid come February. The bumps and bruises from defensive tactics, and my occasional falling from the monkey bar, or rescuing a dummy (which was as heavy as I was) from a simulated burning building, were of minor concerns to me at this point. If I were to succeed, I had to endure the run, regardless of the temperature. Period.

By the second week, I was secretly experiencing a whistling sound in my chest, and my voice or what was left of it was just a rattling inaudible sound. By the time I survived the third week, I was showing signs of labored respiration, wheezing and other conditions during running which resulted in me making my first trip to the Police Physician. At any other time in my life, I would have been happy to receive medical help and advice, but on this occasion, I dreaded the outcome. The physician performed various tests and despite a serious look of concern on his face, he summed up my condition as being mild Congestion. He provided me a note, enclosed but not sealed, in an envelope to take back to the Academy.

As soon as I was out of his sight, I removed the note from the envelope and tried to read it. It seemed as if he along with all doctors, had a special way of writing which presented to be a challenge for other people to read. However, I deciphered the words: Recruit... Pneumonia.........activity......three days. I didn't see anything about my coat or the weather, and he hadn't mentioned anything to me about Pneumonia, because I distinctly remembered him saying mild Congestion. I got the gist of his semantics. It was pure psychology. Recruits should never feel as if they were too ill to function by using complex medical terminology to describe the severity of their illness. While the Academy should be made aware that the potential existed for said Recruit to collapse at any given moment during a seven-mile run.

During my second conference while turning in my Doctor's note, I learned that I was to continue running, but that I should sit on the sidelines when instructed to do so during the running exercise for the next three days, after which I should return to the see the Physician. I was also made aware that continued sitting on the sidelines would result in an assessment of me continuing my enrollment in the 98th Session of the Academy. I was between a rock and a very hard place. You tell me to sit, but if I sit, then I could potentially be thrown out of the Academy? I prayed for a miracle not to show any cause to sit too frequently during running. After my three days, I returned to the Physician for follow-up and to my surprise and a little feeling of relief, I saw another Recruit in the waiting room.

After getting another note with the words: Three additional days.........resume normal... I waited patiently outside for the other Recruit to hear his diagnoses. It was the first time in my life that I was celebrating with someone over the fact that we both shared similarity in sickness. He was happy for his first three days of sitting occasionally on the sidelines with Pneumonia, and I was ecstatic to get what seemed like an extension. We were both instructed not to engage in any conversation during sitting on the sidelines, as speaking indicated that we were in perfect health to continue the run. It seemed, if we were caught speaking, then the instructor would enforce the rules governing mild congestions and physical exertion, and send for an updated note from the Physician in case anything unexpected occurred. We gave each other occasional smiles of relief while sitting and I know I was appreciative either to the Physician or to whatever was responsible for my condition.

After resuming normal training activities, I practiced incessantly on my off-time to run, and I made a conscious effort to show some respect and tolerance for the winter. My future depended on it. Regardless of how hard I had tried, I was still coming down with frequent respiratory conditions which hindered my already challenged capabilities to run long distance. Not too far into the program, I began to console myself that if I was in fact chasing anything on foot for seven miles and was unable to catch it, I was going to consider that it was indeed lucky and that it got away. So, I did my very best just to qualify in this daily seven-mile Olympic event, while trying even harder to surpass the qualification guidelines for my other areas of study and training. My logics paid off and as an added bonus I am now able to see winter as what it is. I wouldn't say we have a love-affair, but our relationship is now quite amicable and without rancor.

Apart from ensuring that I was successful in building a good tolerance and respect for the winter, the police department also did its part to ensure that Recruits who were assigned to Mt Vernon, were also building the tolerance necessary to face other realities once we left the Academy. For starters, the department made it very clear that we should not expect any ease of mobility in responding to emergency situations while conducting patrol duties. Each department represented among the Recruits, was responsible for delivering squad cars to their Recruits, so that we could complete the Emergency Vehicle Operations Course (EVOC), as part of our training. On the day of EVOC, the city delivered a few cars to be used by us during this qualification exercise. Once the cars were driven unto the course, the instructor advised the Mt Vernon group that our squad cars were not in compliance with New York State's regulations regarding motor vehicle operability and road safety compliance. In other words, the police cars could not pass the State's guidelines for Inspection and were dangerous to be on the road. Hence we would not be able to complete this aspect of our training, provided that the department exchanged the vehicles in compliance with the Vehicle and Traffic Law. The department sent a swift response back to the Academy, to utilize the squad cars which were sent, as no other cars were forthcoming. Nothing was said about the Recruits who were supposed to be at the helm of these vehicles, as that was a non-issue. We were expected to find a way through problem-solving to stop these squad cars in the event the brakes failed at ninety miles an hour. Imagine the irony and the back and forth between the Police Academy administration trying to lecture the Mt Vernon Police Department, about complying with the law. I was not even certain if one could have written the other a ticket in this case of Police policing the Police. It appeared though, that they both arrived at some amicable solution to the problem, and I suspect that the agreement was that the Recruits could just be collateral damage if anything serious occurred, because the instructor subsequently directed us to take the course using the previously condemned vehicles.

Upon entering the squad car assigned to me, I was a bit timid to maneuver it over fifty miles an hour due to the uncertainty regarding the condition of the brake pads. The instructor, sensed my trepidation and advised me in a stern voice to, "floor it."

I said a quick prayer for him, (not for myself), because I was already covered from the times I had prayed about the seven-mile run. I wanted to make sure this instructor was consecrated and we were both headed to the same place in this unpredictable vehicle. I followed his direction and floored it. At about seventy miles an hour or thereabouts the car began to sound as if it was going to fly apart in sections, leaving the two front seats in mid-air like a roller coaster. The instructor demanded that I stop the vehicle. He was unaware that I had prayed for him, and it appeared he knew just where we were headed without adequate prayer and forgiveness. I immediately began to comply with his demands but short of pumping the brake pedal repeatedly, the car seemed as if it had a mind of its own. It took a while to arrive at a complete rest, and the instructor exited. His agitation was understandable, but I knew that his intention to call Mt Vernon would have only increased his frustration. In no time he returned to the vehicle, visibly more agitated than when he had left. Someone from the administration there, who was responsible for their fleet of squad cars, told him to go do whatever he felt like doing, (not to the car), but to himself.

In order to complete the emergency vehicle operations, course, I borrowed a vehicle from one of the Recruits who was from a more affluent police department. Their cars still had the seats wrapped in plastic the same way the dealer had delivered them to their respective departments. It turned out that I was fortunate to have received this premature experience with failing brakes and uninspected squad cars, because not very long after leaving the Academy I had my very first experience involving stopping a flying police car, which was not equipped with brakes.

I had started out the morning on patrol, in snowy weather. About five minutes into the drive the windshield was covered, and I realized I needed the wipers, but they were inoperable. That was minor, so I quickly solved that problem by occasionally stopping to use a piece of cardboard to clear the snow from the glass. Less than an hour after being on patrol, the engine came to a halt. I radioed for the mechanic or a tow truck, and the mechanic showed up fairly quickly, with the large rubber bumper affixed to the front of his car in order to push mine from behind. This mechanic slammed the rubber bumper against the rear bumper on the back of the disabled car and began to push. Each time my car would skate on ice away from him, he would increase his speed and ram his bumper against mine once more. He was supposed to have a radio in his car whereby he could communicate with me, but he had turned it off. I kept trying to tell him, that the level of ram was not necessary as the road-way was slippery, but when he did not respond, I realized he could not hear me over his disabled radio.

We proceeded along the way towards the garage, and as soon as I was approaching a steep incline at North Fifth Avenue and East Sidney Avenue, he sent me flying down the hill with one of his unnecessary rams. I tried to brake by doing the pumping action I had employed in the Academy, but nothing worked. I was headed directly downhill into traffic going both ways in front of me on icy road surface. I called out to Dispatch, advising that I was about to crash as the brakes had failed. I wanted to make sure that an ambulance was being sent, once I completed this collision I was planning to engage in. My problem solving skills had kicked in fast. I quickly surveyed the vehicles which were crisscrossing in front of me at the bottom of the hill on Gramatan Avenue, and picked one which appeared to be sturdy enough for a good impact. The vehicle I had chosen was a new Ford econoline van, white in color. I swerved directly towards it, and slammed my car with precision right into its side. The driver of the van was unhurt, and the department employed its own problem-solving skills with regards to his vehicle.

We had learned some of the most important techniques and skills while in the Academy, which would become a central part of our survival, and now we were ready to part ways and employ them in our respective departments. In addition to our new found skills, some of us had even found wives and husbands during our training and inter-actions together as well. But most of all, it was important to carry with us the social intelligence or skills which had been riveted in our heads. Those who neglected to carry these skills with them, were destined for trouble.

We were each going to different places. Some were graduating to places such as Bedford and Chappaqua and places with names which were difficult to spell. The second phase of the training was on-the-job Field Training. Directed by a Field Training officer in real life-situations. His first instruction to me was to forget most of what I had just learned in the Academy. Any running which was required would be over and done in a few min-utes give or take. The most important thing which was to be remembered was situational awareness. Surviving in Mt Vernon demanded most of all, an understanding of the social contexts or situations which I would find myself in for the next twenty years. Understanding the ways in which such situations would shape my behavior and the behaviors of those who were involved in it, was all I needed. I was a master at interpreting things cor-rectly over the life-span of my career.

Seven

THE ELEPHANT IN THE ROOM

My career in law enforcement was embedded in a system of justice that has remained seriously flawed in so many ways. It was difficult to separate the genuine responsibilities of the *service* from the expectations and demands that the *system* imposed.

The attempts to separate the two created a professional tripolar affective disorder. For me: citizen, cop, immigrant. This trifecta collectively represents the top three of many such personalities. Immigrant also includes black. An extension of that list for me, and by no means less important, is female and liberator of a group of people. The liberator was the messiah of victims. Most cops in the system suffered from affective disorders. Though immigration may not be immediately symptomatic of many who suffer, careful analysis of the blood will detect a history of that trait. The majority will never admit their personal list, and I will explain why later on. Every cop's list is different according to upbringing and other factors, and every cop has a different order in which the list is ranked or prioritized. This is true regardless of race, age, gender, color, ethnicity, religion, disability (yes, cops have disabilities too), national origin, or sexual orientation. This is a complex situation, and herein lies my perspective of "what the hell is going on" across the country (not with immigrants alone, as some may believe).

Having the diagnosis previously described is by no means professionally debilitating, nor does it preclude anyone from performing objectively and without prejudice in a law enforcement job. However, the problem arises when we fail to accept that it does exist, when we are unable to effectively balance and control these multiple personalities, and ultimately, when we fail to get help to keep them in check. We literally play mental and physical hopscotch among our respective roles that the system imposes.

The expectations and demands of the system require that all who enter adapt a superhuman persona in order to carry out its ever-changing, never-ending demands. The system requires that we respond to and solve all the ills of the social services along with the specific requirements of the job. The roles and responsibilities are insurmountable, even by superhuman standards. But the system insists on its members maintaining a steady hand and steady mind regardless. If the mind succumbs to the pressure, the feebleminded are on their own. No longer a member. The revocation of membership is gradual and is equivalent to public shaming. It begins with the stripping or removal of all symbols (I'll tell you how important these are later) affiliated with the system. So in actuality, the system strips its member naked, right before the eyes of everyone.

This may not seem like much to someone from the outside looking in, because such a person believes that the fraternity sings "Rock-a-Bye Baby" for every member no matter what the situation. With a little insight from the inside, the brotherhood separates itself from all exposures of any member who has been "certified." Affiliation with such a member may create the unintended but professionally deadly branding that either you also need certification (birds of a feather) or you are in opposition to the system. Either branding is a career choice that no member wants. It is similar to hearing your obituary read while you were still alive.

The talk about and assumption that a cry for help comes with anonymity, discretion, and dignified treatment is entirely and hypocritically false. So allow me to put that hallucination to rest. Exposure is immediate. First, because the seeker is obviously made naked and placed behind a desk in plain sight, in a position where only a pile of paper or the handset of a telephone may cause harm to himself or others. Secondly, because everyone looks on with that judgmental stare that says, "Approach with caution." That being said, no one seeks help, so the affected few are ticking time bombs on active duty.

Once the certified has been restored, the label remains. Restoration, by the way, does not necessarily mean cured, and it most certainly does not mean full reinstatement of membership privileges and affiliation. It simply implies a return to active duty (with a gun).

No one, at least not anyone I have met throughout my career, was ever willing to cry for help when the respective roles (their trifecta) and prejudices were engaging in an all-out war of conflict. Even a war as obvious as the one portrayed in the *Three Faces of Eve*, by Thigpen and Cleckley. The personalities debated issues from time to time, and that was natural, easy to control, and human. All you had to do was change the order in which you ranked them and deal with the situation at hand. But a sure sign (frequently overlooked) that help was needed was when you placed them in order and they kept moving out of place. That is, going bat crazy within the confines of your head, with your finger in close proximity to a trigger.

Everyone, including those entrusted to recognize the problem and sanction help or removal out of the system, made subtle remarks and innuendos about who they saw as being in total warfare with their respective personalities, roles, and prejudices. The next step in the process was that a permanent label of "crazy" was affixed to the individual cop. Not "crazy" with concern, but "crazy" with banterful warning, for others to expect anything at any given moment.

The system institutes psychiatric evaluation as part of the vetting process. But truth be told, not everyone in sound mind with all their prejudices under control can do the job of a cop. So everyone is sane during the hiring process, according to the psychiatrist who approves you for hire. There is no reevaluation after all the personalities and prejudices are evoked as part of this affective disorder. In some places, such as the city in which I worked, this evocation can present within the first week of exposure to the battlefield. I previously described the city in order to create an understanding that this new idea floating around that Zen and Yoga may be able to cure this situation is purely bogus. We cannot put such a responsibility on Zen and meditation. Zen is for stable-minded people who want to remain that way, and who are not thrown off mental balance by social issues of this magnitude.

Remember, these personalities are dormant or repressed during the hiring process, and hence they go undetected. But, alas, they are awakened when the demands of the system set in. Some new ones are also born when theory (from the academy) which applied to places like Bedford and Chappaqua, becomes practical for Recruits assigned to work in places like Mt Vernon. And to be fair and clear, there are many Chappaquas, Bedfords and Mt Vernons nationwide.

Yes, I know the idea of diversity and sensitivity training and such the like are flying around loosely as a cure-all for these types of issues. But diversity training (I'll tell you about those trainings in a little bit) is not an effective remedy to erase any prejudices that people harbor. For prejudices live within the hearts of humans and channel to the brain via the bloodstream. Some prejudices transform themselves into full-blown hatred, while others remain just our personal sources of immunity and defenses. Prejudices are just preconceived notions without any facts to back them up. Blacks and whites alike harbor them.

The things that we experience, that we see on a daily basis—our ignorance, our upbringing, and the things that we are taught through brainwashing or radicalization—are what determine whether prejudices become hatred. The system does not proactively take into account any of these factors. Members of other systems may have similar stories in which they observe their system's failure as well. But that's their story to tell, of how one could be honorably discharged by one's system and suddenly and without warning become dishonorable. That is, if we believe such a change is sudden.

As far as diversity training courses, at least the ones that I had the privilege of attending, they provided a snippet of insight into the differences among cultures and social groups. But their content was elementary, and so if you were present in school for a basic social sciences class, then you could as well have skipped it. The instructors were familiar with the culture embedded within the system. Most were, or are still themselves, cops. The room was filled with cops of all colors and creeds. But there were few cops present from that banter list. Everyone was cautious and guarded. No one wanted to address any specific elephant in the room or any particular hot-topic concerns, so instead, instructors emphasized the need to treat everyone as equal under the law. We promised to do so (pinky promise), and we went right back in full service within the community. The banter-listed ones headed to the speakeasy to cleanse their heads, and the whispering about them began all over again. Before we left the room, we were encouraged to place suggestions into a box about how the program could be improved—I imagine to make us more tolerant, more sensitive, and less hateful (in case there were any among us). The system patiently awaited the suggestions of anyone who dared to include any narrative that might seem too specific, difficult, or awkward to include in the curriculum. In order to teach any new and improved curriculum would take away from the time on the street, which we needed to play our various roles in aiding other failing systems.

The career is not similar to any other. Our way of interaction was different than the interaction among other people in all the other jobs I have experienced. Things that cops find mainstream and which help them to stay strong, sane, and get through the stresses of taking on the responsibilities that other systems levy on them, are what create the bond between cops. It is not wrongdoing that creates the bond. We share humor and opinion about race and culture which others would not find tasteful or politically correct. I recall one day while responding to the third homicide of the day, with the gunshots ringing in the distance, I was with a fellow detective who shared different religious beliefs and practices than myself. A day which was later informally referred to as "Bloody Sunday." We were always respectful of each other's religion and culture. We were friends. We had lunch breaks together, although we oftentimes did not eat similar things. He would openly frown at some of the things I ate, and I could not even decipher what was on his plate half the time. Anyway, he was in the drivers' seat and as we advanced towards the sound of gunfire, negotiating every corner on two bald tires of our oversized Ford Crown Victoria, I quickly told him of the likely connections between the two prior homicides. He had been home on his scheduled day off that Sunday, and was summoned in due to the day going violently awry. After sharing the quick details, I added that, "I think we should say a quick prayer on this one." My friend and partner, took one hand off the steering wheel and grabbed an empty coffee cup which was in the cup holder. I immediately got annoyed and asked him, "Coffee? Really? Now?

The car was threatening to flip over, the shooting was in progress, and this was now the third one of the day. We were approaching a volatile situation. Later for coffee.

He quickly responded, "in my religion I hold an object to pray to, whenever I prayed."

There was no time to show any understanding of his religion, which was dictating that I put my faith and life for that matter in an empty coffee cup. I would deal with the fall-out later, if there was one and I was still fortunate to be alive to do so. I said, "wha?" and grabbed the cup from his grasp, leaving just enough time to say, "Lord have mercy on us," as the car screeched to a halt and we flew open our doors and exited. Later on that evening, when the dust settled, we looked at each other and began to laugh hysterically at what another person, not standing in our shoes, would have probably viewed as my total disrespect for his religion. We later shared this event with some of our fellow detectives and everyone saw the humor in it, absent the disrespect. This action of mine towards this empty cup, would not have been done in the presence of anyone who was not involved in a life and death situation with me. The common thread and bond between cops is life and it's always present alternative as we race from call to uncertain call......death.

An interesting television series called "Shades of Blue," which is on hiatus until next season, depicted a real-life explanation that can help to dispel the idea that wrongdoing is widespread among cops, and that we share a universal bond in covering up for each other. In the series, a female detective was being interviewed for a position in a rogue unit involved in graft; and she was specially selected because she was known to have participated in prior corruption. The unit commander wanted no cop who was too honest to compromise his unit, and finding someone he could trust was extremely difficult for him. If this idea was at all accurate about cops, then his job at handpicking a tainted cop for his unit, would have been much easier for him to have accomplished.

That being said, we have all left the diversity training and are now on active duty. The majority are fine in dealing with the various personality roles and prejudices that arise. We keep them in check, usually with humor, camaraderie, understanding, and the golden rule from our upbringing. We know how to unwind off duty responsibly and in a healthy manner, with Zen. We make ourselves familiar with the communities we serve, and some of us may even reside there. We do not feel disrespected when people don't at first use their government names to identify themselves, because we understand how people may feel that the various systems of government have let them down. We understand that we are symbolic of said government. We quickly adjust to the system's demands and don our social worker hats.

For me, it may even require that I place the immigrant's hat on top of that one as well, and take a quick trip down memory lane to paradise, just to get the government name that I seek. Now we both have each other's government names. We can move on to the business at hand. We are thick-skinned, well trained, emotionally stable, and know just how to handle our various roles—savior, mighty counselor, prince of peace, and cop. The psychiatrist was right about us—the majority of us.

Remember the ones who left diversity training and went to the speakeasy? Well, they are still wearing the cop hat. They're not flexible enough to switch. And the realities of the job are turned up for all of us. It's like a control group and an experimental group, with no one in the system paying attention to or recording the findings. Both groups are continuously exposed to the same triggers day after day, night after uncertain night.

We rush to homicide scenes and witness the last breath leaving the blood-covered bodies lying on sidewalks. We shamefully continue to serve while some among us are depicted on videos shooting unharmed civilians without a cause. We respond to parents who curse at the question of why it took three days to report a twelve-year-old child missing. We get stuck by hypodermic needles and require periodic testing for diseases. We rescue the homeless from extreme heat and cold. We respond to a biological son raping his biological mother. We respond to a jealous husband shooting the maid and his six-year-old child in the forehead. We respond to a father raping and impregnating his biological fourteen-year-old daughter. We respond to drugs being used and sold on street corners. We respond to a brother having sex with his biological mentally challenged sister. We respond to suicide by hanging and other methods. We respond to a baby, killed while being stopped from pooping with a foreign object in the anus, by an angry boyfriend of the mother. We respond to shots fired and stabbings on school grounds. We look down the barrels of guns aimed at us by people we have arrested dozens of times for gun possession. We dodge bottles and rocks being pelted at us. We return to our cars to find the tires flat after responding to calls for help. We perform CPR on the guy who punched us in the face a day prior. We respond to toddlers dropping through windows while the mother lies in bed drunk. We respond to reports of robbery of drugs and cash from drug dealers. We respond to congregations fighting inside churches. We watch our fellow officers get shot and killed for trying to help the community. We respond to multiple people shot and stabbed on the dance floor of a baby shower. We are spat on and told to go and perform deviant acts on our mothers and ourselves on a daily basis. We monitor daily school dismissals due to fighting after school. We conduct truancy checks and are cursed out by the parents and truants alike. We respond to suicide by cop. We respond to barking dogs and neglected animals. We respond to landlords providing no heat and hot water for tenants. We respond to nursing home abuse. We respond to wild animals with their heads stuck in cans. We respond to the mentally ill. We respond to people threatening to jump or who have already jumped. We respond to hospitals calling for help with violent patients that their security officers cannot handle. We respond to calls from social workers to assist them in removing children from their homes. We respond to drug overdoses. We respond to single mothers dropping off unruly teens at the station and vowing to accept arrest, rather than take them home, and the kids sleep in our offices overnight on the desks, because children's services refuses them also. We respond to children bringing loaded guns from home to school. We respond to animals being set ablaze. We are held accountable for dispensing the proper amount of medication in stopping drug overdoses, and in operating life-saving equipment such as defibrillators, in the correct way.

Just to name a few.

There should be at least one thing included (never mind the entire list) that can help to shed a little light on what can occur as a result of repeated exposure to these elements by some already mentally fragile, system-neglected, pinky-promised-diversity-trained-cop, who had prejudices growing into hatred before the exposure to the elements.

Feelings, perceptions, emotions, and weaknesses lay dormant or are deliberately kept under wraps until they are awakened by practical exposure and interaction with the things or people feared, hated, or perceived as threats.

Eight

PRODUCTIVITY, ECONOMICS, AND THE WONDERS OF THE JUSTICE SYSTEM

There were many days when having played my roles in my prescribed personalities specifically during my patrol years and feeling extremely productive, my satisfaction was erased by the fact that the productivity sheet required for submission at the end of the tour was not completed. This was a way to calculate specific activities performed in the community in terms of revenue. There were no columns on the sheet for citizen interaction that had not resulted in revenue. Neither were there any for the kid who had asked me to turn my emergency lights on for him to see them. He had only seen them when the car screeched to a halt in his neighborhood streets to take someone away in handcuffs. This moment of productivity, of giving such a kid a chance to see the lights, may have illuminated a path of hope in the future for him.

But the perception of productivity, from a system's point of view, is purely economically based. The criminal justice system was, and still is, a business. One of the biggest industries there is. One whose commodities are people. Refer to the Department of Justice Report on the Ferguson (in St. Louis County, Missouri) Police Department online.

The demand for these marketable goods branded as damaged is intertwined amid philosophical thoughts and teachings that translate into "protection and service." The service is in fact moving the commodity from the community. The marketplace for trading is correctional institutions, which, by the way, have blossomed into economic privatization. Which means that private companies headed by profit-driven organizations have seen the prospect of economic success and have come to invest in the commodities being traded for a profit.

This shifting of the justice system toward inclusion into the group of Fortune 500 companies is indicative of the fact that the justice process operates in an assembly-line fashion. It competes well with some of the major automobile manufacturers, except their commodities are cars, and we deal with people. There are still those who are resistant to accepting the mere explanation of this as a social science of economics that fits into the production, distribution, and 'consumption' of goods and services.

The acceptance of this fact does not negate any argument that for some, the trade is necessary in preserving the lives and safety of the rest of us, especially vulnerable children. It is a necessary system, no different than the pharmaceutical companies that sell one drug capable of curing a rash, but that will cause blindness, kidney failure, internal bleeding, erectile dysfunction, infertility and possibly death. Rest assured, the same company also recommends that you talk to your doctor about blurred vision so that they can also sell you the drug for that as well.

The justice system has become so lucrative that the concept to transfer ownership of people is taking form in modern-day society. I marvel at the concept of economic privatization, since the revenue gained from trading people does not exceed the cost, especially when we think of the wasted minds and the more dangerous commodities unleashed on society once people are recycled through probation and parole. I often ask myself if the money, time, and effort spent to meet the system's quota would have been better spent by us as taxpayers trying to correct or even prevent some of the damages arguably created by social injustices in the first place. Especially those damages that manifest themselves in early childhood years and in disadvantaged upbringings. And those agents like Lead, that deliberately run through our pipelines in such places like Flint, Michigan or into the water coolers of our schools. Instead, deportation and privatization have become the Hail Mary for our economically driven system of justice. The problem is they are not full of grace.

Consistent with the economics is that the use of statistics has become so commonplace in measuring the success of criminal justice programs that people have become numbers. There is emphasis on the number of arrests made in an attempt to keep a federal or state grant for a community. Emphasis on the amount of revenue brought in by the police department. Emphasis on the number of beds required to keep a private prison in operation. Just like smoke follows fire, in the same way, money, corruption and power are inseparable. And it is money that causes the confusion that we see between power and authority. If we use numbers to represent people, then soon we will no longer see people, even when they are staring right at us.

Another characteristic of the system that never ceases to amaze me as a Jamigrant is that a call to jury duty excludes legal aliens and beckons the participation of citizens only. This remains, despite the fact that defendants have been convinced that the choice of a jury trial will be constitutionally granted with a jury of their peers. The judge's responsibility is to interpret the law. The question then remains, does the learned judge have any difficulties interpreting the law for a legal resident, or does the legal resident have some type of foreign mental deficiency in understanding the judge's explanation? One thing remains certain, and it is that defendants may be from a pool of citizens or noncitizens alike, so as an awakening, the jury pool is not representative of everyone's peers. This is evident that some are compromised in a deviant manner from the utterance of the word go. Just in case the argument of not allowing legal resident aliens to serve as jurors is the fact that they are not a part of suffrage, then frankly, those naturalized as citizens who participate in the voting process merely exercise this democratic right based on the promises and stance of politicians. Legal aliens are capable of gobbling up political campaign promises as well. This deliberate exclusion of some from making decisions in the criminal justice process is perhaps one of the first signs of inequality. But alas, these same individuals who are unqualified to be jurors are very qualified to serve within any of the armed services of their choosing.

The other issue regarding the system that I found to be quite hypocritical was the promise in the Miranda warning directed at the poor: "If you cannot afford a lawyer, one will be provided…" Well, in actuality, the wrongfully accused and the rightfully accused will be appointed a lawyer from a set of well-intentioned people. Their caseloads are so heavy that they cannot be blamed for the system's failure in not affording them the breathing room to even familiarize themselves with their clients' names. Hence, it will continue to take life sentences before the innocent is exonerated, as we don't even know their names. So for the poor, it's easy to get into the system, and darn near impossible to get out. Many times while waiting at the courthouse for cases to be called, public defenders are double-checking the name of the accused that they are there to represent. They had no advance time to familiarize themselves with a name, much more to plan a proper defense strategy. But the justice system foresaw the problem of heavy caseloads and preemptively rectified that matter with plea bargaining, which it distributes in abundance like cotton candies of confectionery justice. Hence a common justice system saying, "whoever talks first, gets the sweeter deal."

Carefully positioned on the list of wonders experienced within the system is the emphasis, importance, and power of symbols found in different components of the justice system, (remember I had promised to tell you how important these are?). Symbols have always been important to human beings in general, and oftentimes say who we are and what our mission is. In fact, my own religion demonstrates faithful attachment to the powerful symbols of the fish and the cross. This system that I speak of is no different; it is comprised of people whose actions are influenced by symbolic references. The judge's robe is a sweeping reminder that Your Honor's personal opinion and prejudices have been objectively swept aside. The gavel represents order, or conclusion of what Your Honor has decided. The officer's badge is supposed to be a symbol of rank or affiliation, while the uniform of the law enforcement officer, among other things, is a visual symbol or representation of the profession, authority, and designation of an official status, which is designed to garner conformity in response. These symbolic representations and others have been understood by all, except presumably for the poor legal alien, who has been deemed incompetent to understand the judge's charge to serve on a jury.

However, the symbols do not end within the components of our justice system; they extend to the citizens as well. You see, the system places a high level of importance on symbols and assigns a few to the people who conduct justice-related business with it. As learned scholars and writers, McNamara and Burns in their book titled, Multiculturalism in the Criminal Justice System, quotes social scientist Jerome Skolnick as defining what is meant by the term, "symbolic assailant." The system, in particular police officers, hold a certain perception of what the social scientist calls the "symbolic assailant"—namely, the symbols of the potentially dangerous person or assailant. These are the perceived sources of violence or enemies to be reckoned with. In the book, they are referred to as persons who use gestures, language and attire that policeman has come to recognize as a prelude to violence. Well, we just looked at all the symbols of the justice system's participants above. These symbols are all things they wear or use and carry on their persons in the performance of their duties. Which brings me to deduce that the identity of the symbolic assailant could be associated with some form of garment or the way it is worn below the backside. Remember, symbols reveal who we are and our purpose. It is obvious that the power of symbols runs the whole gamut of the system, from Your Honor on down, so there is a sense of equality within the system with reference to how judgment is cast.

This sense of equality gave me pause, though, and revealed yet another wonder, because "equal" does not always translate into fairness. Many astute scholars have also expressed their criticism for this imbalance between fairness and equality. Considering the bail of, say, one hundred dollars of an average middle-class defendant who has been arrested for a minor offense. Then consider bail of an equal amount for a comparable offense, for a defendant who collects glass and plastic recyclables and arduously pushes them in a cart to the dispenser station. In short, disregarding criticism for lack of political correctness, this defendant picks up bottles and cans for a living. The system ignores the obvious fact that such a defendant is economically challenged and offers him or her the same bail as the previously noted offender. The treatment is equal, but the question of fairness embedded in the system still lingers. How do we separate the equality and fairness within a *justice* system?

There are legitimate cries as well for the system to hold those charged with wrongdoing, notably cops, accountable. That takes me to the duties and responsibilities of the office elected to legally represent the people. Such a task requires me to briefly revisit Greek mythology. To be specific, the story of Pandora's Box, or rather, Pandora's Jar, out of respect for aliens of Greek descent. The Greek are very particular on the issue of jar or box. So let me begin with the *case*: The consequence of opening the box or jar in Pandora's case is well-known, as we may recall it from our various areas of elementary studies. As a quick refresher, the evils of the world taunt her as they escape the box.

However, one part of the story that we so often fail to emphasize is the content that was at the bottom of the box. Did you forget? Ok, hope was sitting in the bottom of the box. If we remember that hope for change exists therein, then all fears to open the box will be allayed. Which brings me to the *point*: The prosecutors' offices within our system of justice are faced with the daunting reality that any conviction involving wrongdoing in the performance of public service could possibly require a review of particular cases (boxes) previously sealed shut with the evils of the world locked away in them. Remember, these boxes were packed in good faith and tied with a ribbon and bow of indubitable trust. Yes, trust (more than transparency) is a common ligament that exists between our components of justice. It binds them together with never-ending mutually beneficial agreements. Cops who purposely commit wrongdoing could not have begun on the first day they were caught. Our system of justice should guarantee independent assistance to these elected officials in opening the boxes if the need should arise, so that they can rest assured and prosecute without fear, favor, or concern for poll results. Remember how effective it was back in the Academy when the Police tried to police the Police?

Prosecution lest we forget, does not end at the indictment stage of the process. As one former New York State Court of Appeals Judge stated, (prior to his own indictment), that prosecutors can indict a "ham sandwich." After he made the assertion, one mainstream media outlet noted that the former Judge believed, "the Grand Jury operates more often as the prosecutor's pawn than the citizens' shield." With that said, indictments seem to merely appease the spirits and calm the uproars. It has become the pacifier of our justice system which we spit out after some of these trials.

The other wonder of the system to me, was the astronomical degree of responsibility and authority entrusted to the police and the degree of judgment faced when forced to use this authority in the quagmire of decision-making. The ultimate decision anyone could make would be to take the life of another human being. Once done, it cannot be undone.

Every single individual in society who is in a position to one day make such a decision regarding someone's life has fortunately been afforded time in advance to ponder it. The judge, when faced with the task of presiding over the jury deciding on the penalty of death, goes into chambers and, I am guessing, sifts through the many files of case laws, carefully evaluating mitigating and aggravating circumstances. Then before charging the jury, the judge perhaps clears his or her mind of any prejudices that sympathy or past experiences may have evoked. This clearing of the mind can usually be accomplished with a hole in one or a long walk. In the event uncertainties still exist, then Your Honor may adjourn the proceedings and take as much time as is necessary, just to be sure.

The jury gets to deliberate—engage in long and careful consideration. This is usually accomplished over pizza, sandwiches, salads, and discussions with fellow peers in a conference-room setting, and then perhaps off to their hotel room if they are sequestered. In the event that any misunderstandings or questions arise, the jury gets a chance to request to see what was already shown to them.

Oh, let us not forget the governor, who is oftentimes charged with this decision as well. The governor may at leisure during the course of tenure think about just who will be pardoned and granted clemency, and at the end of a long elected term of service, gets the chance to come to a calculated or an informed decision to spare (or not) the life of inmate number six-sixty-six on death row. The leisure of time at their various disposals is everything.

I remember sitting on a jury for two weeks and felt honored to have seen both sides of the coin. Though it was not a jury responsible for any decision about the death penalty, we were still charged with making an important fifty-million-dollar decision. I was the only one on the jury who was a detective, or in law enforcement for that matter. I kept observing how everyone was getting flustered trying to arrive at a decision. They had previously made me the foreperson on the jury. I was calmly making a list for everyone's lunch that we would have delivered. Sensing my demeanor, a man asked me how it was that I was so calm amid the stress of arriving at the decision. I explained to him that I was accustomed to making quick decisions under stress, but since I had the leisure of time, I was going to calmly use the time to make my decision and make it right. They had the time and comfort, yet they had become so flustered.

Even though cops are trained, the fact remains that they are still humans. With that being said, I saw where police officers were criticized unfairly when they made an error during exigent circumstances. Whenever the outcome was good, they were lauded as heroes. Whenever the outcome was bad, they were villains.

Nine

Dead Wrong

For a significant part of my career, my experiences were much like the well-researched documentaries on law enforcement work. The story lines depicted in many drama series that dominate the electronic box to which we have become so addicted are all false.

Those unbelievable events where everything goes as planned, with high-speed chases and shoot-outs, ending with court cases resolved within an hour; no productivity sheets or reports to complete; and perps confessing to crimes before being given complete immunity from their present and future criminal acts—all of these are false.

The anomaly where investigative cases are solved in an instant, because the forensic lab technicians and the medical examiner are just waiting patiently and in readiness for the call—not true.

The aberration that district attorneys are always visiting crime scenes before they are properly photographed and cleaned up- purely propaganda and is entirely misleading.

Press conferences where the media is being told that the police is actively searching for the suspect in any case except a serious felony-on a scale of one to ten, where ten is the biggest lie which has ever been told to mankind, this falls off the chart and is definitely an eleven.

In fact, the notion that things are always done quickly and in a hurry can be dispelled by one of the earliest career experiences I had as a newcomer.

I was charged with the task of checking on the welfare of an individual who had not been seen or heard from for a few days. It was during February's malicious reminder that way too much fun was had during the previous summer months. I can't recall exactly what manner of fun I had engaged in over the preceding summer months, but remembered clearly that I was praying for forgiveness for the enjoyment of said activities. I arrived at the location of dispatch and received no answer to my knock. After carefully positioning my inquisitive self on a concrete ledge under a window and peering through the foggy glass, I could see what at first appeared to be a man sitting somewhat upright on a couch, wearing a hat precariously lowered over his forehead. Feeling relieved that I had found the person for whom everyone was so concerned, and more so that he was simply relaxing and enjoying a hiatus of solitude, I tapped on the window to gain his attention.

No response, not even a flinch to indicate an interruption to sleep. Despite my petite frame, I was confident that my knock was powerful enough to interrupt even a state of being in a hypnotic trance, so I began to observe his paunch, which was thinly covered by a button-down long-sleeve dress shirt. After careful observation of his midsection, I realized that there was no movement there, and immediately summoned for medics and others responsible to breach the door. Now being able to observe him up close and personal, it was obvious from the early signs of rigor mortis that his disappearance from his normal daily activities and socializations was not intentional. Paramedics presumed he had been in this state of mortality for several days.

Further investigation of his surroundings showed no signs of foul play, and an initial observation of his medical supplies and prescription bottles provided a clearer insight regarding his health. It was clear also that the pharmaceutical companies had a vested interest in him. With obviously nothing left for anyone to do for him—and for me for that matter—I was left in his company to await the arrival of the county's medical examiner. On TV the coroner was always on the scene within seconds, and the autopsy was done during the commercial break.

Upon calling the medical examiner's office, a voice mail recording in his stoic monotone voice directed callers with remains awaiting retrieval to leave a brief message indicating the caller's name and title, location, department's telephone number, and the identity of the deceased if known. It should be noted that the deceased, many of whom I did business with, conveniently did not possess identifications on their persons. Even in death they still opted to give you a run for your money, playing the "guess who I am" game, "because I'm not going to tell you." But this was one of the easiest identifications I ever made since enough information, along with photographs, were all over the residence.

Anyway, I recorded my message and prayed for a timely response from the goodly coroner to my department. To help pass the time, I began to watch the snowflakes fall and accumulate on the trees outside the window that I had previously peered through, which landed me in this situation in the first place. I began to wonder how long I would be left in the present company of one who had gone to the other side.

A silent hour went by, with just thoughts of what my company was experiencing in this second life. Was it snowing over there? Was he looking down at me, wanting to take me with him to this beautiful place in the clouds? What was he thinking of this strange woman who had peered through his window; broke his door lock; took off his hat, which he had tilted on his head; brought strangers inside; and then took up residence when everyone else had left? I radioed my department's dispatch and inquired if the coroner had left an estimated time of arrival to retrieve the remains. The friendly young lady radioed back with an explanation that due to inclement weather, treacherous road conditions, plus several other remains to retrieve, he was likely to arrive in another couple of hours. A quick calculation of the one hour I had already waited plus the guesstimated additional two hours made me resign my mind to take a seat in the only other chair, located directly in front of my host. We stared at each other, passing the time in our separate ways of being, both oblivious of what it was like being in the shoes of the other. I could only imagine his, and he could no longer imagine mine.

After about four hours, which seemed like forever, the coroner arrived alone and requested my assistance in carrying the deceased to the vehicle, as the wheeled stretcher could not maneuver the snow-covered, unplowed surfaces between the vehicle and the residence. It seemed, though I did not care to ask, that all the bags had been used up on the coroner's way to my location, and so a white sheet had to be utilized to wrap the remains.

As we walked toward the vehicle, the right arm, propelled by the stiffness of the rigor mortis, flipped upward from where the sheet had been folded along the side and slapped me, without any provocation on my part, along the side of my face. It was a clear indication to me that I was not the only one disappointed with the pace at which important things are accomplished; even the deceased often grew impatient with us as well.

On many occasions I saw where the youngest and most vulnerable among us often suffer similar frustrations of poor service at the hands of this stronghold, even when it remains the only venue of justice and protection on which they depend. And oftentimes the justice system and systems of social service are not in sync with what is needed for this vulnerable population.

I recall being summoned by the school system about the allegations made by a seven-year-old that she had suffered unthinkable acts at the hands of a pervert, whom her mother had hired to watch her in lieu of available or affordable after-school programs. The mother, it appeared, had a part-time job during irregular hours and chose to withhold some of the money she was receiving for child care (from the other system) so that she could afford this unlicensed caretaker of her child.

This animal was not concerned about the rate of pay, as long as the mother would deliver her most precious possession to him after school about three evenings per week. The child had suffered too much of this, was no longer able to succumb, and, I imagined, told her teacher just about the time she was dreading to leave school to be picked up by her secret monster. The education system contacted the justice system, and professionals from other related systems also came on board.

I became a semi-permanent fixture in her life, as I was present for most of the meetings and evaluations that followed. We developed a bond, which I noticed would win me a smile or an occasional hug from time to time when her trust level of human beings was a little unguarded. The innocence that her years indicated was in total conflict with the thoughts this predator had placed inside her head. She demonstrated this conflict through her language and vivid description of what she believed were the proper names for the human anatomy.

By all accounts, I believe that she was destined to be the poster child for the system to prove its mission and redeem itself in protecting and servicing the vulnerable under its care. And I bore a huge chunk of this responsibility in making this happen.

I truly believed that some significant part of this responsibility was nearing a close when one of the system's representatives asked the victim to explain how she felt as a result of the horrors she had described. In her own way, she explained that she felt like jumping off the tallest building to alleviate her pain.

At this point, my hands were tied. The systems that had been brought together to correct society's ills began tripping over one another. One system representative immediately decided that such a statement indicated a threat to harm herself or others, and therefore would require all other systems to take a backseat. Another learned representative beckoned for paperwork to be drawn up so that she could immediately be taken to a place to get the required help under lockdown.

The facility in question stipulated that no inquiries be made about her, due to the Health Insurance Portability and Accountability Act. Her mother, who had failed her in the first place, began to scream at all the system representatives present. She blamed me personally for all the systems' failures. I was accustomed to taking the blame for everything that occurs in society, so this was no different. She didn't know that without access to the victim, it would get even worse, as I was helplessly dealing with the fear of this monster being left to roam free. Furthermore, committing the child to an institution could potentially be the defense's dream whenever she was released to tell her story. The system placed great emphasis on mental illness but only when it related to credibility.

Being forced into a strange place indefinitely and without warning, and by those who were supposed to help, would cause anyone to develop animus against such a system. God knows to what dark places that animus could lead the mind as she developed into womanhood. The system demanded that I solve a problem, but it had tied my hands firmly behind my back.

There was an elected office, I quickly recalled, that we had in place to help people, so I immediately reached out. "You have a problem," I was told. Hell, yes. Not that I needed anyone to tell me this, and the real truth was that the problem was also that of the person speaking to me. We were in the same system and shared the same responsibilities to this child, but oftentimes did not operate with the same motive.

"Well, the victim's credibility has been shot, and winning this case is darn near impossible unless you could find another victim who could corroborate." Now my feet were also tied, because I had already walked and checked out all his known contacts, and they had produced no additional victims. Did I have to get two victims or more for the system to help me? Besides, "winning" just sounded like a game, or someone's personal little satisfaction that they craved.

The next suggestion stunned me to the core. "Well, build a case against the mother for negligence so we can bring this case to a close." That's how the system works. The victim would end up in another unfamiliar place whenever she was released. How would she feel about the three systems to which she had turned for help? More importantly, how would she ever forgive the one (me) who took her mother away and left the monster to roam free? I refused to carry out any such act, on the grounds that pinching pennies and stupidity had caused her to look for cheap child care, and that if the predator struck in the future, she would never cooperate with the system again. These were the types of people who harbored hatred toward me and the system.

I felt sick and helpless in the place in which I was wedged. I would have essentially become the system's pawn in helping to victimize this child three times over.

Ten

On the cusp of my retirement, I was transformed by some of my experiences with the declining quality of leadership within the career. The period marked a set of leaders who were opposed to forward thinking in a rapidly changing world. The most effective way to explain the system's continued dilemma in retaining them, anywhere in the country for that matter, is through Matthew 9:17: "Neither do people pour new wine into old wine skins. If they do, the skins will burst; the wine will run out and the wineskins will be ruined…"

The community is able to sense poor leadership, and so under these types of leaders, the criminal elements in the city during that time ran amuck. The gangs had a BOGO (buy one get one free) promotion on firearms, and ammunition must have been free also, because I was unable to find enough buckets to secure the spent shells left at each crime scene. They sold extended guarantees to the buyers that they wouldn't be caught.

The leaders adopted every trait of the three wise monkeys. At one point they seemed to have added a fourth monkey, which covered its derriere. A slot on the popular television series "I Almost Got Away with It" dedicated in their honor would have been an appropriate culmination to their tenure.

Under their leadership, there were morning shellings, afternoon shellings, evening shellings, and night shellings among the other variables with which we had to contend on a daily basis. They would know the exact locations and times when shootings were going down and the date retaliations were scheduled to take place. Under their watch, a typical morning when they arrived at work would start something like this:

In walks the captain at 10:30 a.m. He was due in at 8:00 a.m.
Q. How many shootings did you have last night?
A. Three shootings. But thanks for asking; I'm OK. One victim is at Jacobi
Hospital.... (he interrupts).
Q. It was supposed to be four. What happened to the other one?
A. I had three. Was there informa... (he interrupts again)
Q. Can you get that bucket of shell casings on your desk to the lab? We need to

see if they'll match the shooting scheduled for next
Friday night.
A. Yes. Who is the projected shooter for next
Friday night and what are the
details about this planned shooting so we can pick
him up today?
Q. Pick him up for what? We don't have enough.
A. We could speak with the person who told you,
so we can get enough.

In walks the Lieutenant, and he overhears the tail-end of
the conversation.

Lieutenant: Perhaps we should wait to see if he
changes his mind. People do have a tendency to rethink
their actions. Let me check the schedule on his last fifteen shootings and see if they occurred on schedule. Talk
with the district attorney to see if sixteen will be sufficient
to avoid a plea bargain for reckless endangerment. And
uhhhhh, let's see. His gang is supposed to be meeting
at the playground on Thursday night to distribute the
equipment they need for Friday. I'll, uhhhh, try to get
a copy of the minutes for that meeting, and then we'll
regroup and have our own meeting.

Our computer system, burdened by the frequency of newly
generated cases, seemed to have run out of case numbers
to assign to the various incidences of insurgency. At one
point, the system began to flash a response that, "this incident has just been assigned a case number; see your IT

administrator." They were happening so fast the computer thought we were logging the same incidences back-to-back.

The leaders came up with a usually genius idea that was utilized back in the early seventies. They had no answers for anything related to decision-making regarding the actual problem of the increase in crime. Instead, they retreated backward in time, determined to keep things just the way they were. "Perhaps we should start logging the cases in this ledger." So, lines and columns were drawn in a twenty-pound ledger, due to computer overload, for everyone to start recording shellings. Imagine resorting to primitive scrolls to record incidences of crime in a technological age, because deficiency in leadership skills fell short of producing more viable alternatives, to stop the shootings in the first place. There was a song I had learned in paradise, and it would resonate with me during this regime: "Old time something come back again."

The epidemic grew, and they purchased two more ledgers. The clergy of the biggest skyscraper congregation located in the middle of the city joined with other clergies and called for an immediate cease-fire. Enough time to allow us to process the crime scenes, get fresh bottled water, and purchase nonperishable foods. The state stepped in, and the county loaned a helping hand as well. But the latter did not put many troops on the ground. In fact, they explained the decision in coming to our aid or rescue as being to gather intelligence for us.

Their method of acquiring such intelligence was to assist in making jump collars or, more politically correct, to conduct sweeps related to vice activities and the like. Regardless of what it was called, it involved the collaring of hundreds of prostitutes and johns, with the hope of getting actionable information from them. Initially I was part of the fingerprinting and booking team for these misfits.

Like any other offenders of the law, they too were entitled to a telephone call to advise a loved one or an attorney that they were in custody. I delivered some of those calls for them during the fingerprinting and booking process.

I tried very hard not to tell the many wives and girl-friends who picked up the telephone at home the reason why their dear johns were in custody. For those who demanded to know and demonstrated any form of hostility or lack of respect for me ringing their number so late at night, I would slowly and carefully deliver the news in its entirety, up to the point of climax in the story. Of course, not omitting the part where the beautiful cars registered in the names of the wives had been towed and secured as evidence of the conduit of the crime. Paying for the towing and storage of these cars used as brothels was just another blow added to the emotional cost of the degrading proclivity of their husbands. But for the city, the revenue from towing was priceless.

So, after patiently listening to their insults about ringing their telephones, I would explain to them that I was sorry to have disturbed them with the news, but their husbands had asked me to notify them about court proceedings in the morning due to whatever he was caught doing next to the baby's car seat in the back of their Mercedes Benzes. For once, I was not the bad guy. The system was appropriately blamed this time for charging so much to have the cars released to their respective owners.

But we didn't need any more intelligence than the amount which seemed like it was already available, due to the accuracy in the predictions of the events. These perverts didn't have any intelligence to proffer. We were under siege.

County flew overhead, generously lit up the battlefield for us, and refrained from landing, perhaps out of fear that their drone would be jacked by the insurgents. County being in the sky was like an air show, as the drone was doing all kinds of maneuvers, flips, and darts to get from one area of shelling to another. The victim's vehicle, being followed to the hospital, detoured and became the suspect vehicle, now being sought in retaliation for the original incident.

Around my twentieth year, I met the victim of the last case I would investigate. He was a young man of average stature, hardworking, humble, and incidentally a Jamigrant. I remember the fear in his eyes as he sat trembling at my desk, telling how he had been kidnapped, beaten, placed in the trunk of his car, and robbed at gunpoint a day prior. He was forthcoming with all the answers to my questions regarding the events of his frightening ordeal, and I had no trouble in feeling his authenticity and thereby believing him. He showed me his paystubs and his checking account statements, with all the consistent direct deposits from his company. He was a workingman. He spoke of how his mother pushed him to file a police report despite the suspects threatening him against coming forward.

My only criticism of him was that he presented to be a bit timid and not a ragamuffin in nature, given the fact that he was taken in and out of the car trunk several times by his captors and never once tried to escape. Too submissive, considering that the typical Jamigrant would have put up a little resistance to the idea of being locked in a trunk, gun or no gun. Once you allow us to come out of that trunk, to check the ATM, we are not going back in. We are extremely claustrophobic and have a tendency to become very combative when cornered or forced into anything.

Other than that, we are very nice people. I didn't allow him to feel my disappointment in his lack of ragamuffinness, as it would have been highly inappropriate to blame or criticize the victim. I had to help him. He was a true victim.

After outlining the preliminary investigative steps I had planned to take in solving this case, I received a swift dose of reprimand from another supervisor. For no reason that could be explained to me, the victim's case was unbelievable, and the trail of money he showed was highly questionable. This quickly reminded me that there were a few elephants in the room as well. He spun around on his mobile chair, leaned forward, and explained the following in a very deep voice: "Ninety-nine percent of these types of crimes are bullshit, and this one is among the ninety-nine, so I suggest you do not spend any of your time on it."

Here we go again, I thought to myself, with the issue of time for which the taxpayers have overpaid and the reluctance to give credence to anyone with characteristics dissimilar to thy holy self.

I simply explained that I wholeheartedly believed the victim and had intended to investigate his complaint. I quickly asked if he would like to meet the victim, knowing full well that he would refuse to break his longstanding tradition of highfalutin separatism. He declined the offer, which I had already suspected he would. I asked if there was anything else, and as soon as he said there wasn't, I exited his "upper" room determined to serve the victim. All that was known of the victim was what this supervisor had read in the initial report: male, black, of a certain age, skilled worker, and the account of the incident.

That begged the question as to which of these criteria was used, to include him into this lying 99 percent with money from a questionable source.

So the following days and nights were spent beating the pavement, following every lead, and interviewing every person I could find. The determination to do justice for a deserving citizen who was victimized and left helpless, fearful, and violated was my only mission.

Perseverance paid off, resulting in the identification of the perpetrator. I advised my partner that the case was in fact not among the 99 percent destined for the attic, and I was ready to move toward an apprehension.

The perpetrator subsequently received a sentence of twenty years in prison. I skipped the accolades that followed, as they were meaningless and without value to me. It appeared that others were more needful in using it as a trophy. I saw the relief and gratitude in the eyes of the victim when he shook my hands, and that meant everything. I felt his gratitude that someone within the system had believed him, despite being a part of the 99 percent of those who are often denied justice.

Eleven

Class of 2015

It couldn't have been clearer: the system was on life support and needed an overhaul, stat! The primitive ways of doing things and painting the outcomes with the harsh bristles of utilitarianism, whereby the ends justify the means, had become more and more unacceptable nationwide. The dominant alpha personalities, resistant to change and opposed to transparency, needed to relinquish the reins. They saw no faults in the usual way of defining justice, neither in theory nor in practice. In fact, when called out on any of their missteps and improprieties, they would explain them away just like the old soldier who could no longer march in cadence with his platoon. This soldier, refusing to accept his shortcomings, explained that, "Everybody was out of step but me."

So these old soldiers, who now defined the foundation of the justice system's establishment, were persistent in teaching the same old ways to the newcomers, some arriving already filled with arrogance, embossed with power and braggadocio. This mixture, when garnished with inexperience, hatred, lack of social awareness and mental instability, can be the most toxic, combustible brew.

Many who saw the imminent collapse of a system going awry started to develop an exit plan. It was becoming more and more impossible to change things from the inside. One had to find a way to change the pool of the ones going in. As if all who saw this light had seen it just about the same time, a growing list of well-intentioned veterans who refused to short-change the public were leaving in droves. I made the list. Class of 2015.

Just like an ominous parallel to the establishment justice system, the political system began to create frustration among the masses as well. One system in peril was depending on the other, which was in total chaos, for help. There was trumping for immediate change to make the country safe again, or calls for the start of a political revolution of some kind. Some were being promoted as the law and order candidate to secure the opportunity in the upcoming general elections to bring much needed reform to the system.

However, I decided to contribute by helping to prepare some of the prospective members of the justice system to become a part of that change.

Twelve

Contemporaneously with the chaos within the connected systems and my longing to re-experience some vestige of professionalism, I felt a deep desire not only to write, but also to devote more of my time to something else that could be equally fulfilling and transformative. I had previously returned to teaching about eight years prior in preparation for my retirement from the justice system. Now I had a renewed passion and obligation to continue as an adjunct professor of criminal justice at a local college. My father was thrilled. I was returning to a pathway he had ordained for me and from which I had defected. I needed to reconnect with life and again be able to see the good in humans, as those experiences endured over the last five years or so had not only chipped away at my ability to believe in the integrity of those entrusted to lead, but had also demanded that I help to groom those who would be followers.

The teaching profession was extremely forgiving; I felt its embracing welcome the very first day I entered the classroom.

I had the chance to look at the size of my classes beforehand, and each class roster had over thirty students registered. This was unexpected, as I had imagined a much smaller multitude. I garnered my own style and approach to delivering my lectures, and I could tell instantly when my style seemed different from that of other professors. Homework on the first day of the semester resulted in whispers and other inarticulate sounds of pain, which I ignored. There was no cure to alleviate this type of pain except a trip to the campus library and a conscious effort to free oneself of any texting addiction or social media dependency that might prevail. Having some kind of assignment to quickly assess each student's level of performance was my only intention for assigning homework on the first day of each class. After all, grading four classes of thirty-five papers each would not have been something I would have planned arbitrarily unless I harbored some deep feelings of dislike for myself.

Ethical Issues in Criminal Justice, as one of my courses, breathed life and hope into my desire to once again trust in the direction of my challenged career. My students through their term papers outlined many calls to action, which helped to generate this feeling of hopefulness. Many were astute enough to mention the vetting process as a source of the problem within the justice system.

Of course, there was one student who asked me during class discussion one day, "But, Professor, how can I balance constitutional requirements and at the same time prevent the guilty from going free?" Three things came to mind: judge, juror, and executioner. Instead I said, "You will find it easy if you keep your thumb off the scale of justice." The conjunction "but" at the start of her question, along with her tone and tenor, seemed indicative that she was already struggling with carrying out this required responsibility and obligation. Both her palms were turned upward, and her shoulders were pressed against her neck. Defiance to the constitution. There were many such interesting interactions between my students and myself. I made a note of students who needed reconditioning in certain vital areas of the subject matter. I would prepare extra homework in these areas and assign it to them whenever their grades needed a boost. Only after continuous reading and reasoning were they able to be convinced that we cannot arbitrarily disregard, circumvent, or make changes to laws and precepts. This vital concept, which I was determined to etch in their moral craws, was one that I had digested not only in academia but in the lessons learned throughout my career.

Accountability was another major concept that I intended to drive home in a forceful way. As one politician—excuse me, excuse me, businessman and billionaire—would have said, in a "bigly" way. At the time he said it, the word was retweeted more than a million times, and I didn't realize then that there was a desperate need to have this word at our tweeting disposal, until I saw the deficiency in demonstrating a sense of responsibility among some students with respect to the timely completion of research papers.

Assignments of this nature would even warrant some students attempting every means necessary to switch to another course, especially if the number of pages stipulated went into the double digits. A requirement of footnotes was also a serious event of trauma in their college lives. To alleviate the potential for outburst and to prevent any thoughts of one committing hara-kiri in the classroom, I would post the guidelines for said assignments via the Internet over the weekend and add that said assignment would be discussed in further detail on Monday during class. This way, their parents could deal effectively with the initial loss of consciousness or cardiac episode, and I would deal with the other end after the storm. Nothing beats breaking bad news very slowly, and as a bonus, the Internet created a temporary distance, which was priceless in the event of fainting or other college-related episodes.

Every class had one queen of a student—on very rare occasions it was a king—who had a flare for the dramatic. I really give the academic advisors credit as to the way in which they evenly distributed these particular students among the different classes. The distribution of queens must be meticulously orchestrated because my fellow professors are all blessed with one in their respective classes.

Upon my arrival to the lecture hall on Monday, the only noise detectable was the sound of my five-inch heels echoing upon contact with the glistening tiles polished to janitorial perfection and detail. I give much credit to Vicky, entrusted with cleaning, as the job to keep floors so squeakily polished under the feet of hundreds of people could not have been an easy one. She was a pleasant and hardworking lady, and like myself, she was an immigrant. She always busted out a warm smile whenever we encountered each other in the hallways, and I would snatch a piece of paper towel from her cart to wipe the residue of the chalkboard marker from my hands. I spoke with her in sentences of half Spanish and half English, but we laughed in the same language.

So, reverting to my scholar and queen of theatrics, she would raise her hand, ready to dispute what she had seen on the Internet over the weekend. In anticipation for her objection to the number of required pages for the research paper, I would acknowledge her. "Yes, Genesee, what's your question?" "Oh, Professor. it's Gen-nee-si." Let's try this again, I'm thinking, with the last name this time. The last name had twenty-six letters hyphenated, thirteen on each side. So I disregarded that and moved on to the issue under discussion. Research paper, twenty pages, twelve font, double–spaced, with footnotes in APA format, and then arrived quickly to the due date for the assignment.

This was the day of reckoning, when accountability would be reinforced. I announced that any assignment submitted one day after this date would be subject to a deduction of ten points, and two points on each day thereafter. Points are necessary in the teaching of accountability at the college level, as they can seriously disrupt the grade point average and significantly affect the transcript. I ignored all sounds of conniption and distress and proceeded right into the lesson of the day.

On the day of reckoning, the temperature of some of the papers was noticeably warm to the touch—a clear indicator that said papers had just been extracted from the printer, and the ink was still in the process of drying. I put the warm ones on the top of my pile for extra special attention during the grading process.

It makes the rest of us wonder, what is there to think about in college dorms besides homework assignments and how to be accountable? But with the proliferation of tweeting, blogging, face timing, and live streaming, homework becomes obsolete, and the professor who demands it becomes a pain in the derriere of twittering students. Omg! Some would rather text one another a million times regarding the complexity of the assignment than to actually complete the assignment, Lol!

As small as the dorms were, if I should inquire from one student whether her roommate was in the class next door, the student would tell me, "Professor, I texted her this morning, but I didn't get an answer." I had to maintain a straight face when grasping the concept that a text was sent from one to another in such a small space as a college dormitory. But more frightening was the concept that no follow-up was done to ensure that the person lying there on the bed in the dorm was OK.

Another challenge facing scholars of the millennium is having a plan B in the event of Wi-Fi connectivity issues, which sometimes occurred within the classroom environment. This technology-dependent, Silicon Valley-inspired population is only equipped with stylus pens and e-books accessible via touch screen tablets. I often wondered how inconvenient it could really be to have a pen with ink and a few pages of ruled paper to take some notes, instead of snapping pictures of notes from the board. Not a thought I would have considered politically correct to have expressed openly, as that could signal an opposition to change. Political correctness is a sore point also with this generation. Forward thinking is important, and the professor must remain mindful of this fact.

During lectures, one must be cognizant of the need to remain objective, truthful and as neutral as possible on all issues that are trending, as any comment taken out of context lands one on YouTube, with a million hits. Religion, politics, sexuality—these are the issues that are hot buttons within the college environment. "God bless you" is a no-no, as atheists make up a large percentage of the college population. The words "trump" and "wall" in the same sentence could stir up a demonstration on both sides of the issue. Neutrality, inclusivity, and tolerance are the professors' creed.

So in adhering to political correctness and my foregoing creed, I would choose a more subtle way of showing
the ink pen-deprived populace that they should be better prepared. I informed them that attendance could not
be taken via the computerized roll call venue. Wi-Fi was
down, and IT was working on it. Hence I would be cir-
culating a ruled sheet for them to write, yes, write, their
names and identification numbers to record their presence. After the announcement, I pretended not to watch
their reaction. A few had a double-edged stylus, so the
entire class of thirty-five pen-less undergraduates would
wait to borrow one in order to sign their names on the
attendance sheet.

It was always imperative regardless of their inability to
equip themselves with a functional pen to record their
attendance, since they had chosen dates carefully orchestrated when they would have emergencies.

On these specific emergency absences, I would get
e-mails advising that the absence was unforeseen. During
one semester alone and after several assignments past
the deadline, one undergraduate sent three e-mails concocted in text lingo. The first one read, "Sorry will not be
in class for few days due to a DIF." It took a few minutes to
digest the gravity of the situation, as a death in the family
is extremely traumatic. After expressing my condolences,
the first time, and then my deepest condolences the second time, I began to wonder on the third occasion if any
family members were left and whether they had taken
the homework assignments with them on their journey.

They coincidentally chose this journey on the same dates assignments were due.

Upon this student's return to class, I guess after he buried the homework assignment, I carefully inquired with politically correct demeanor what family member this was, just so as to determine if it was the same one from the prior e-mail. I could tell he did not wish to jinx any particular member of his family, as he was vigorously searching his brain for a name and title.

My sarcasm kicked in, and I informed him with seriousness and empathy that the loved one would have been proud of him being strong amid the grieving to complete the overdue assignments.

One art I had learned well along my previous career path was to maintain an expression on my façade that could not be easily connected to what was on my mind. There is nothing more noble and important than carrying out the wishes and expectations of the dearly departed, I explained to him. I further seized on the opportunity to explain how important it is for all of us to engage ourselves even with the distraction of assignments, in order to prevent sadness from taking residence in our thoughts, especially when we are going through a period of grief.

After just a few semesters, it became imperative to develop a mastery not only in delivering the lecture, but also of adapting the mind-set of a master manipulator, where you shift the balance of power occasionally from those who present sorry excuses for not completing overdue assignments.

Not that the various incidences of realization brought on by my return to academia were not eye-opening enough; my eyes popped clean out of my head when I actually realized the extent of an underground organization being run by some of the students of the A-list.

The organization of which I speak was nothing short of something fit for the movies. The A-listed students would complete various assignments for the F-listed students for a fee, which was calculated based on the complexity of the assignment and the due date. The price began at a minimum and skyrocketed if the assignment was due within twenty-four hours of placing the order. Other criteria included number of pages, types of sources to be used for reference, format, style, and font.

The idea of the fraud was one thing, but the level at which it was thought out was quite another.

Determined to test the extent of this operation on campus, I devised an impromptu exercise to understand the similarities between this business and the dark web. From face value, it appeared the two shared the same elements of exclusivity. I quickly gleaned over all the names associated with calculated DIFs and various other excuses related to overdue assignments, grabbed my lime-green highlighter, and went through their assignments meticulously, drawing a line through any idea, word, or written thought, phrase, or theory that I deemed to be complex for those having more than one DIF per semester.

During my next class session with them, I calmly announced that I had received some very interesting research papers, the content of which I would be calling on the writers to do an oral presentation to the class. My first student was summoned to the podium, and just as he thought he was going to read the paper to his fellow classmates, I threw a monkey wrench right into his plan.

Shifting my black frame glasses to the tip of my nose and peering over the rim, I advised that he was only required to expound on the highlighted areas, after which I would open the floor for questions to be directed at him. I made sure he understood that I had a few questions of my own concerning the highlighted areas. My lips pursed. Glasses were sitting just right. Patience level was heightened. The sound of silence was extremely loud. I waited. During the wait I decided to read the body language, which is always a dead giveaway. The brow was beading up in little shiny balls of what appeared to be sweat, despite the room being reasonably cool. The hands clung to the sides of the podium as if for dear life. The eyes were darting back and forth from left to right of the highlighted paragraphs. The moral compass was pointing due south. There was no doubt: this was a product derived from the organization, and I suspected that the price was substantial. I took a moment to break the sound of silence, just to announce that failure to verbally explain any theories presented in the research papers would result in a failing grade and that any student who wished to dispute such a grade would be required to sit through a meeting with the dean and yours truly.

As if the suspected issues of plagiarism, fraud, deception, and possible money laundering weren't damning enough, the dean, suspension, and possibly expulsion were now added to the list of consequences for collegiate indiscretions. The dean, I might add, in my guesstimation, was about a half inch shy of reaching my five foot three height, but was no pushover, despite the smile on her face that always preceded a moment of chastisement in her office. She would welcome you in her situation room with a loud voice, and then drop her pitch a few decibels for the duration of the "read." Her pronunciation of words and her overall command of the English language made you feel obligated to listen attentively to what she was saying. Her stern manner of enunciation made you feel certain that you would never repeat whatever action had brought you to her presence in the first place.

So after my decision to invoke the rod (an applicable syllable in her surname), I called one after another to the podium, with the same dear-in-headlights expression on their faces, appearing to behold their papers for the very first time. It took me about five minutes afterward and a red ballpoint pen to inscribe a large F in the top right-hand corner of each paper. I then sent around a ruled sheet daring anyone who wished to dispute the grade to add their name to said sheet. The ruled sheet came back to me untouched, with not one single solitary name written on it. This indicated that everyone recognized that their behavior was deserving of their grade, and that the behavior fell under no other category that "F."

The new assignment in lieu of the Fs was posted via the Internet that night. The number of required pages was increased, and the due date was deliberately set for the day following the next scheduled exam. Hashtag accountability. The next class session, everyone acknowledged that they had read the new assignment, and that they fully understood it. We moved on.

I always tried to begin the classes with a few minutes of whatever was trending in the arenas of politics and justice, or just any social events in the news. We were never short on topics. I was sure to watch CNN, or read the accounts from other mainstream media sources, if even for five minutes a piece to hear what they had uncovered each evening. I was ready with a topic even when my students had been chasing Pokémon all night. Plus, they had their mobile devices on vibrate, that were supposed to be turned off during class, so they could always quickly read something and act as if they had made themselves familiar with it the night before. I was familiar with all the tricks, but I acted oblivious. Never showed my hand in the classroom, it is the best strategy to ensure that I remained in the know.

So while the political madness was trending among the candidates in the primaries, I took a moment to engage my students in a dialogue regarding the vacancy of the seat on the Supreme Court. This seat was really of grave concern to me, because there were so many issues that needed to be addressed, and putting them on hold was just not fair to the American people. States had begun to pass laws regarding who could use what restrooms, and important stuff about immigration and a wall was being discussed; same-sex marriage and same-sex divorce were also on the list. The presidential candidates were also giving their respective speeches on activities of terrorists (refer to other books, not this one, for the name of any specific group).

Besides, November was quickly approaching, and the situation of the seat would suffer yet another set of uncertainties. The size of Justice Scalia's shoes was conservatively a size twelve, and someone had to fill those shoes. Deciding to test the temperature of the millennials with respect to this issue, I dropped the projector from the ceiling and presented a photograph of all the justices donned in their revered black robes, with one seat left void by the untimely absence of Justice Scalia. We had to discuss their respective backgrounds quickly.

For a good while, it felt like the night before Christmas in the classroom. Not a student was stirring, not even a mouse. I garnered some patience from the fact that even Justice Ginsburg herself had dozed off momentarily during the Papal speech and almost pitched forward out of her seat during the President's State of the Union address. Everyone gets a little bored sometimes. The problem here was that some people by virtue of a thing called tuition could not afford to be bored, and incidentally could not afford anything because of the amount of the tuition. My glasses were hung on nose bridge. Waiting.

I noticed little flashes of light all around the room. Millennials were connecting with their devices to tell me why this boat on the projector screen was wavering to and fro, tipping its balance conservatively to the right and liberally to the left, while the American people remained nauseated sitting in the stern. The answer as to why this empty seat was so important was not forthcoming; I needed another modality.

OK. I told them President Obama had named Chief Judge of the US Court of Appeals Merrick Garland for consideration. "Look up his background on the various devices, and tell me why the president suggested him. Also think about the size twelve shoes he was going to put on." While they were checking, I was praying for Judge Garland because I suspected his was going to be a long wait when Senator McConnell heard about "Obama's audacity to pick" in an election year.

Miss Brown told me that his background said he was a centrist. Good. We were getting somewhere, albeit slowly. But what did this mean for the rest of us with blue lights shining from the devices in our faces?

Yes, the term liberal-conservative, and how the decision in filling the seat, could affect the arbitration of Justice in America had to be understood by everyone quickly, so we could move on. My next move could land me in the dean's office if I was not sensitive about any atheists who might be in the classroom. I took a chance and told them about King Solomon and the two women who had claimed to own the one baby. How the king sent for a sword and threatened to split the baby down the middle. They immediately realized that in this case, it was a donkey and an elephant that were in dispute. We moved on to the course work from the textbook, but not before I had to quell a disturbance that was brewing in a corner. Supporters of Hillary and one of Donald's supporter, and some who were feeling the "Bern," were coming to a head. These minor disturbances could escalate; the professor had to be cognizant of topics that could start a movement and end up in the hallways. The president's office was at the end of the hallway, and the director's was located a few doors before his. Nothing escaped her, always pleasant with a bright "good morning" seeking me out at exactly eight forty-four and thirty seconds, before my eight forty-five class on a Monday morning, pretending to be interested in whether or not I had an enjoyable weekend. I guess she was unsure if I was still prone after all these years to act on island time.

A reminder of the research paper's due date could stop this heated discussion before it canceled out my lesson and had the director heading down the hallway. So I reminded them of it, and it was the night before Christmas again.

I knew exactly what emoji they sent one another across the room to express their feelings about responsibly meeting the deadline of the paper, but there is a matching letter grade for whatever emoji was texted.

I kept posting links on the web that had relevance to this project, causing their cellular telephones to go off with notifications every time the "submit" button was pressed. This reminded them about responsibility and accountability.

An emoji wasn't the only venue in which these millennials expressed their opinions of the professor and the assignments and content of the syllabus. They were given their own venue by which to spread the word. At the end of each semester, professors got a link on which to click, so we could read the feedback at our leisure.

This feedback told what could be improved for next semester, or it could tell if any major problem was brewing about King Solomon and the baby. I always reminded myself that a negative comment in one of the feedback about homework assignment, most likely meant that more was needed to continue the lesson on responsibility and accountability.

Before reading the feedback, it is highly recommended that a glass of wine be consumed. It is best also to do this after the grading of research papers, to ensure that any comments read do not unduly influence the grading process. Sometimes it's pretty easy to tell who wrote what.

So at the end of the semester, I accessed the website and clicked on the evaluation link, which took me straight to the portal of comments. The first one warned everyone contemplating taking this class not to do so if they did not like talking in class. "She (meaning me) makes everyone talk despite the fact that not everyone likes public speaking." I took two sips and carried on, because I thought we were in college to talk. Another comment said, "I learned much more than I had expected in this course, and the material was challenging, but she made it easy to understand." OK, note taken; I will need to raise the expectations of students next semester, as it seemed from this comment they were expecting too little. There is a problem when we expect little in life. Next: "She (me), among other things, changes the due date on assignments." I stopped reading and turned my glass almost upside down, with my head tilted backward. This was one of the students from the dismantled organization involving the bogus research papers, still in denial as to what entailed fraud. This student had not yet accepted responsibility. This student was still telling the world that I kept changing the due date, instead of saying a new paper was given to replace the F for the fraudulent paper.

I kept reading. All the other comments could be addressed with added homework or other curriculum-related adjustments. There was just one student still struggling with these two principles. Responsibility and Accountability.

So far, I was making progress.

Author's Biography

M arie Bell-Mack was born in Buff Bay Portland, Jamaica, but she spent most of her childhood in Moneague Saint Ann, where she attended Ferncourt High School. She then went to Moneague Teacher's College and taught at two schools: Watsonville Elementary School and Moneague All-Age School.

In the late 1980s, she immigrated to America. There she received a bachelor's degree in psychology from Fordham University and a master's degree in public administration from the John Jay College of Criminal Justice. In 1995 she joined the City of Mt. Vernon Police Department, where she worked for years, eventually retiring as a detective. She was the first Jamaican woman in the department.

Bell-Mack is currently an adjunct professor of criminal justice, and *Jamigrant: The Story of a Jamaican Immigrant* is her first publication. She lives in New York with her husband.

www.ingramcontent.com/pod-product-compliance
Lightning Source LLC
Chambersburg PA
CBHW060622290526
45793CB00001B/109